Step by Step Guide to

INDIAN COOKING

Khalid Aziz

Hamlyn
London New York Sydney Toronto

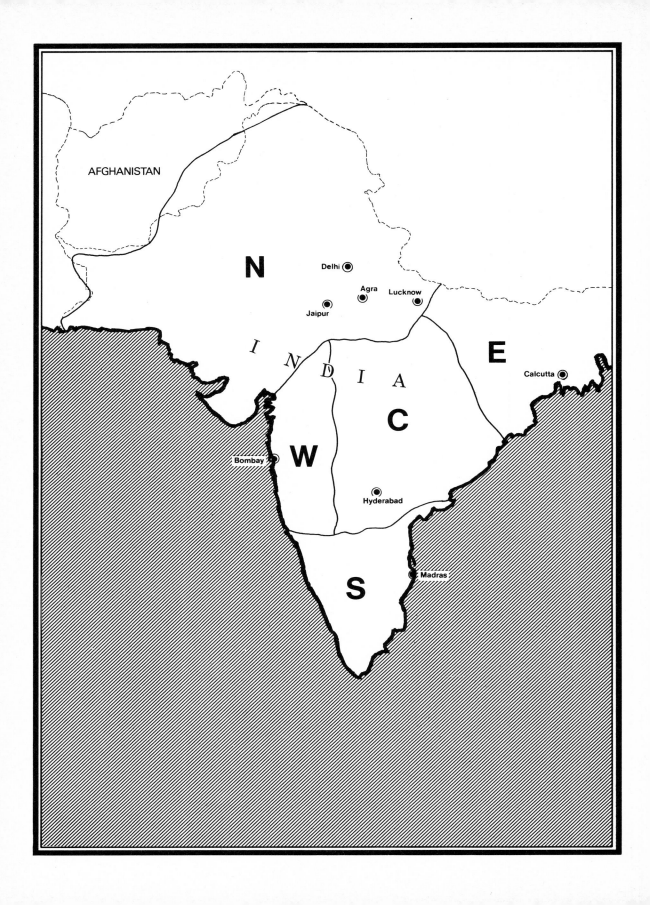

CONTENTS

Published by
THE HAMLYN PUBLISHING GROUP LIMITED
London New York Sydney Toronto
Astronaut House Feltham Middlesex England
© Copyright 1974 The Hamlyn Publishing Group Limited
Tenth impression 1983
ISBN 0 600 38093 9
Printed in Italy
Photography by John Lee Line drawings by Jackie Grippaudo

ACKNOWLEDGEMENTS
The following colour photography is by courtesy of J. A. Sharwood and Company Limited: page 32
Dishes and accessories used in photography kindly lent by
Indiacraft Limited, Oxford Street, London.

USEFUL FACTS AND FIGURES

NOTES ON METRICATION

In this book, quantities have been given in both metric and Imperial measures. Exact conversion from Imperial to metric measures does not usually give very convenient working quantities and so for greater convenience we have rounded off metric measures into units of 25 grammes. The table below shows recommended equivalents:

Ounces/fluid ounces	Approx. g. and ml. to nearest whole figure	Recommended conversion to nearest unit of 25
1	28	25
2	57	50
3	85	75
4	113	100
5 ($\frac{1}{4}$ pint)	142	150
6	170	175
7	198	200
8 ($\frac{1}{2}$ lb.)	226	225
9	255	250
10 ($\frac{1}{2}$ pint)	283	275
11	311	300
12	340	350
13	368	375
14	396	400
15 ($\frac{3}{4}$ pint)	428	425
16 (1 lb.)	456	450
17	484	475
18	512	500
19	541	550
20 (1 pint)	569	575

Note When converting quantities over 20 oz., first add the appropriate figures in the centre column, *then* adjust to the nearest unit of 25. As a general guide, 1 kg. (1000 g.) equals 2·2 lb. or about 2 lb. 3 oz.; 1 litre (1000 ml.) equals 1·76 pints or almost exactly $1\frac{3}{4}$ pints.

Liquid measures The millilitre is a very small unit of measurement and we felt that to use decilitres (units of 100 ml.) would be easier. In most cases it is perfectly satisfactory to round off the exact conversion to the nearest decilitre, except for $\frac{1}{4}$ pint; thus $\frac{1}{4}$ pint (142 ml.) is $1\frac{1}{2}$ dl., $\frac{1}{2}$ pint (283 ml.) is 3 dl., $\frac{3}{4}$ pint (428 ml.) is 4 dl., and 1 pint (569 ml.) is 6 dl. For quantities over 1 pint we have used litres and fractions of a litre.

Tablespoons You will note that often measurements are given in tablespoons; the spoon used is the British Standard measuring spoon of 17·7 millilitres. **All spoon measures are level**.

Oven temperatures

This chart gives the Celsius (Centigrade) equivalents recommended by the Electricity Council.

Description	Fahrenheit	Celsius	Gas Mark
Very cool	225	110	$\frac{1}{4}$
	250	130	$\frac{1}{2}$
Cool	275	140	1
	300	150	2
Moderate	325	170	3
	350	180	4
Moderately hot	375	190	5
	400	200	6
Hot	425	220	7
	450	230	8
Very hot	475	240	9

NOTES FOR AMERICAN USERS

In the recipes in this book quantities are given in American standard cup and spoon measures as well as Imperial and metric measures. The list below gives some American equivalents or substitutes for terms used in the book.

British	American
dough or mixture	batter
frying pan	skillet
greaseproof paper	wax paper
grill	broil
kitchen tissue	paper towels
liquidiser	blender
muslin	cheesecloth
minced	ground
stoned	pitted
whisk	beat/whip

INTRODUCTION

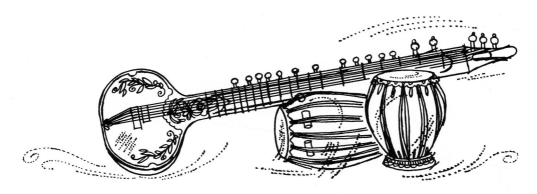

To anyone setting out for the first time to cook Indian food, there appears to be a myriad of regional variations with which one has to cope. In an attempt to make things easier, I have set out the recipes simply according to the points of the compass. You will find chapters on North, South, East, West and Central India. This is not to say, however, that those of you who know your Indian cooking reasonably well will not find your old favourites.

PLANNING A MENU

I have tried to make the individual chapters as comprehensive as possible and by combining the recipes as advised in the summary at the end of each chapter, you should be able to produce an Indian meal representative of the area covered by the chapter. I would strongly advise those of you who intend to entertain guests with these recipes to ensure first of all that you are familiar with the techniques involved in the preparation of each dish. Of course, this will mean that your family will become guinea pigs for all your attempts at curry-making, but this is far better than trying to cook too many unfamiliar dishes, and perhaps having a disastrous time when it comes to entertaining your guests.

To begin with, try to keep within the recipes mentioned in each chapter; this will minimise the risk of producing the wrong combination of dishes. Once you are confident of your proficiency you can start to juggle around with dishes between the chapters, in fact you can produce some very pleasing combinations as long as you follow the rules of common sense. For example, if you are serving rice, do not serve great mounds of chapattys or parathas as well. When you serve these breads, do ensure that they are freshly made as there is nothing worse than a soggy chapatty!

A lot of people are put off by the hotness of Indian food and will often use this as a reason for not eating it at all. Many a time I have heard the phrase: 'I'm a meat Madras man myself', said as proudly as if the speaker had endured a fate worse than death; but I feel that I must dispel this notion that people in the Western world have about the Indians. It is true that some of them like a good deal of 'kick' in their food, but most, quite sensibly, go for flavour. I think it is flavour that you should be aiming for when trying to emulate the Indian way of cooking. For this reason, it is very important when entertaining guests to ensure that you have a combination of dishes whose varying degrees of spiciness complement each other. Thus, your guests will be able to choose what they prefer and you will be able to satisfy not only the 'fire-eaters' but also the steak and kidney pudding men.

MAKING YOGURT

If you are at all worried about harming your guests' palates with hot, spicy food, then one of the best standby antidotes is plenty of simple, plain, home-made yogurt. The last few years have seen a tremendous increase in the popularity of yogurt, and today one finds it in many forms and flavours. But I think it is true to say that the yogurt that is obtainable in plastic cartons in supermarkets, bears no comparison with the yogurt that is sold by the dood wallahs in the streets of India. Yogurt-making is another subject to which a great deal of mystique is attached, presumably to promote the various yogurt-making devices that are on the market. It always amazes me when people say: 'I simply can't make yogurt, it always goes to water', because really yogurt-making is the easiest thing in the world; there is nothing to it.

Yogurt is basically milk that has been turned sour by the action of various bacteria. In theory, as these bacteria multiply very quickly, it is only necessary to add a starter dose of the bacteria in the form of some already made bacteria from a shop yogurt and after a while you will have your own. In practice, as many of you who have tried will know, it is not quite as simple as that. This is because there exist in the air, and in the milk, although it is pasteurised in most cases, several other kinds of bacteria, all of which are equally capable of multiplying. So the first step in making successful yogurt is to boil the milk, and leave it to boil for about three or four minutes. This kills off any bacteria that are liable to vie with the yogurt bacteria.

Thus you have prepared a breeding ground free of competitors for the yogurt bacteria. All living organisms have an optimum temperature at which they live best; yogurt bacteria are no exception to this rule and herein lies the secret of good yogurt-making. Once you have boiled the milk you must allow it to cool, and all you need to do is to add the starter dose of yogurt. But this is where most people make their mistake; if you add the yogurt when the milk is too hot you will find that after leaving the milk to stand for the requisite twelve hours you will have an excessive amount of watery whey and a lumpy, cheese-like substance at the bottom of the pot. This yogurt is not suitable for cooking or eating! The golden rule is: 'If in doubt, allow to cool'; it is far better to add the starter yogurt at a lower temperature than one too high. All you need to do then is to set the milk in a warm place in your kitchen where it is not likely to be disturbed for twelve hours. If you have never made yogurt before, I would advise you to start off with just a pint of milk although you will find that some of the recipes, especially the ones from north India, require greater quantities than this.

COOKING UTENSILS

Much has been made of the various cooking utensils which are used in the Indian cuisine but in fact you will find that the utensils are available in any Western kitchen. For curries, all you need is a heavy iron pot and a wooden spoon with which to stir.

In some of the recipes I have mentioned the use of a liquidiser. Whilst this speeds matters greatly, it is by no means essential, and a little hard pounding with a pestle and mortar will achieve the same results, albeit less speedily.

In nearly every case where a specific Indian utensil is used I have found that there is a corresponding Western one, and it is the latter which I have mentioned. What you are trying to achieve when preparing an Indian dish is to impart the flavour of the various spices to the meat or vegetables that you are cooking. This is done by preparing the spiced sauces and in some cases by preparing the meat in such a way that it readily accepts the spice flavours. The skill of the Indian cuisine lies in the special methods required to bring out the flavour of the spices and to prepare the meat and vegetables; it is by no means necessary to have special Indian utensils to achieve this.

COOKING RICE

The cooking of rice seems to be another aspect of Indian cooking which Western housewives regard as a problem. One hears so many stories of how ordinary boiled rice has turned out as a jellied mass which takes hours to scrape off the saucepan that it is easy to believe that one has to be born within the shadow of the Taj-Mahal before one can produce perfect rice. Needless to say, this is not the case as long as a simple rule is observed, that is, always start with good quality rice. By good rice I mean the most expensive Basmati rice that you can buy – it is false economy to buy Patna rice unless you want to make rice pudding! When you have obtained the Basmati rice, all

you have to do is to add the correct quantity (usually one cup of dry rice per person), to double the volume of boiling water and then boil until the rice has softened and there is no hard centre to each grain. Drain off the excess water and transfer the rice to a covered dish and put into a hot oven for 30 minutes. You will now have perfect snow white fluffy rice with every grain separate.

SPICES

The appreciation of spices and their various combinations is an acquired art, and can only be achieved after many, many years of studied blending, cooking and tasting. However, it must be stressed from the very start that the word spicing does not apply solely to how hot the dish is but to its flavour, and as I have said before, it is the flavour that one should be aiming at when cooking an Indian dish. It would be helpful to go through some of the spices and to point out their various functions.

Coriander *Dhania* Coriander is used in three ways: either as the whole seeds; as powder; or as the leaves of the sprouted seed. The powder is more generally used both for flavouring curries and in the preparation of garam masala. The green leaves are used in the minced meat for koftas and kebabs.

Cummin seed *Zeera* Used whole in rice and bread. Powder used in curry dishes.

Red chilli powder *Lal Mirch* This is the dynamite that imparts the hotness to most Indian food. Use with care!

Tamarind *Imli* The pod of the tropical tamarind tree, used crushed to produce a bitter flavour in curries.

Fenugreek *Methi* Used with fish and some meat dishes, mainly to hide smells. Hence its use with seafood!

Turmeric *Haldi* This is the powdered root of a plant which grows in India. It is famous for its bright yellow colouring. When used in curries it colours the sauce a deep red.

Most of these spices and the various other ingredients both fresh and dried, are available at Indian stores in most major Western cities. A number of these stores operate mail order departments for those customers who live in the provinces.

POPPADUMS

Even the relative novice at Indian cuisine will know what poppadums are. Perhaps this is because they are the most bland of Indian savouries and I have yet to meet anyone who does not like them. Essentially the poppadum is a crisp form of bread made from chick-pea flour. I have not included a recipe for poppadums for although they seem a simple dish, they are incredibly difficult to make. I think it is true to say that all Indian restaurants import them from India. This is because when rolling the dough the temperature and humidity are critical. There is a technique even in frying them and it is worth bearing in mind a few points.

You will find that the poppadums you buy from the delicatessen are about four inches in diameter. After frying they should be double this in size. It is essential to keep the oil clean. The poppadums will be quite dusty and the dust will spoil the oil so before cooking, tap each raw poppadum to get rid of the dust. The temperature of the oil is critical. A piece of poppadum should sizzle immediately when dropped in if the oil is at the correct temperature. Use a large frying pan of medium depth and fill it with vegetable oil to just less than an inch below the brim. Heat gently and keep testing the temperature with pieces of poppadum (remove each piece after testing and always use a fresh piece). When the oil has reached the right temperature fry the poppadums two at a time. giving each side about five seconds. By frying two at a time you will prevent the poppadums curling up. The idea is to keep them as flat as possible. Remove as soon as they have reached their full size and stand on kitchen paper edgeways to drain. Ideally, poppadums should be served as fresh as possible but they should be thoroughly drained of oil. In humid weather you may find that even freshly cooked poppadums become soggy. To remedy this, place them under the grill for a few seconds but make sure that you do not toast them.

GARAM MASALA

One of the other combined spices which has been much talked about by Indian cooks is garam masala. During my research for this book I have found that every cook I have talked to has his own special recipe for garam masala and so it seems an impossible task for me to recommend the right one. However, I will now give you a recipe for a garam masala that can be used universally throughout your curries, but by all means feel free to alter the ingredients to your taste. After all, if the Indian chefs can do it, there is no reason why you should not do it yourself.

Note When storing spices, it cannot be too highly stressed that the secret of good flavour is to keep your spices in tip-top condition. You can only do this by using airtight containers for all spices.

IMPERIAL/METRIC	AMERICAN
1 oz./25 g. cardamom seed	¼ cup cardamom seed
2 oz./50 g. ground coriander	½ cup ground coriander
1 oz./25 g. cloves	¼ cup cloves
½ oz. cummin seed or powder	2 tablespoons cummin seed or powder
½ oz. mace	2 tablespoons mace
large pinch nutmeg	large pinch nutmeg

1 Combine all the ingredients in a shallow ovenproof dish and roast them in a moderate oven (350° F, Gas Mark 4) for 20-30 minutes. Allow them to cool and then grind in a coffee grinder or a mortar and pestle.

2 Store the spices in an airtight bottle.

7

NORTH INDIA

A famous food critic who used to write for a London newspaper once said in an article that in his opinion Indian cooking had never reached any real peak. Whilst one could forgive him for this statement in view of the fact that he probably had very little experience of good Indian food, one could not help feeling that he was doing a grave injustice to Indian cooking as a whole. It is true to say that the sort of cooking that has been provided in the average Indian restaurant in Western cities has been far from adequate, but anybody who has ever tasted Mogul cuisine will know that this cuisine is as well developed in terms of expertise and finesse as the French and Italian styles of cooking.

It was the Moguls in the sixteenth century who brought their food to its flamboyant height with such dishes as shahi tukra, roghan gosht and kesari chaval, and it is the Mogul style of cooking which prevails in northern India today. The Moguls differed from the southern Indians in as much as they were essentially meat eaters and thus the cooking of north India shows meat cooking at its prime and over the centuries north Indian cooks have devised many methods of preparing delicious dishes from the various meats available. Thus this chapter on north India contains a number of delicious dishes utilising meat and more specifically, meat prepared by marinating.

ROGHAN GOSHT

The prowess of a north Indian cook is often judged by her ability to prepare roghan gosht. Consequently, there exist any number of recipes for this dish and some cooks insist on lengthy lists of ingredients sometimes over twenty items long. But the secret of roghan gosht lies not so much in the number of ingredients as in the way they are put together.

IMPERIAL/METRIC	AMERICAN
1 lb./450 g. lean lamb	1 lb. lean lamb
1½ teaspoons salt	1½ teaspoons salt
½ pint/3 dl. yogurt	1¼ cups yogurt
2 large onions	2 large onions
8 oz./225 g. ghee	1 cup ghee
2 oz./50 g. fresh ginger	½ cup chopped fresh ginger
4 cloves garlic	4 cloves garlic
¼ pint/1½ dl. water	⅔ cup water
½ teaspoon ground black pepper	½ teaspoon ground black pepper
2 teaspoons paprika	2 teaspoons paprika pepper
1 teaspoon cummin seed powder	1 teaspoon cummin seed powder
2 oz./50 g. tomato purée	scant ¼ cup tomato paste

1   Cut the meat into 1-inch cubes, then add the salt to the yogurt and rub well into the meat.

2   Cover and leave in the fridge for 24 hours.

3   The following day, slice the onions and fry in the ghee until golden brown. Use a heavy 4-pint saucepan for both the frying and the main cooking.

4   Liquidise the chopped ginger and garlic with the water and add to the onions. Simmer for 10 minutes.

5   Add the rest of the spices and simmer for 10 minutes. Add tomato purée and stir for 5 minutes.

6   Then add the meat with the marinade and cook gently for 1¼ hours or until the meat is tender.

Be prepared to dig deep into your pockets for this one, it must be one of the most expensive dishes in the book. You might when you look at the final result, be excused for wondering whether it is really worth all the trouble and expense. I must admit that I have not been very impressed with tandoori crawfish but I include it because many of my friends have enthused over it believing it to be the ultimate in tandoori cooking. In Britain the only way to obtain crawfish is to buy them frozen. Sometimes they are known as 'large prawns' or 'lagousta'. Whatever they are called, you will be expected to part with a fantastic sum per pound of crawfish, including the shells.

IMPERIAL/METRIC	AMERICAN
12 crawfish	12 crawfish
½ pint/3 dl. yogurt	1¼ cups yogurt
¼ pint/1½ dl. vinegar	⅔ cup vinegar
1 teaspoon salt	1 teaspoon salt
1 teaspoon black pepper	1 teaspoon black pepper
½ teaspoon paprika	½ teaspoon paprika pepper
½ teaspoon chilli powder	½ teaspoon chili powder
1 teaspoon garam masala	1 teaspoon garam masala
1 teaspoon fenugreek	1 teaspoon fenugreek
red food colouring	red food coloring
1 oz./25 g. fresh ginger, chopped	¼ cup chopped fresh ginger

For garnish

wedges of lemon   wedges of lemon

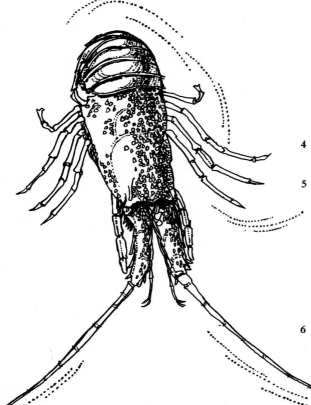

1   If you get the crawfish in a solid block of ice, thaw out by soaking in *cold* water. If you use hot water you will find that the fish will cloud over and some of the flavour will be lost.

2   Meanwhile, prepare the sauce for the marination. Put the yogurt and vinegar into a liquidiser together with the salt, pepper, paprika, chilli powder, garam masala and fenugreek. Liquidise until a smooth sauce is obtained. More red colouring should be added until the sauce is quite red.

3   Put to one side and turn your attention to the crawfish which should by now have separated. The heads are usually removed by the fishmonger and the body left with six legs dangling from the shell. If the head has been left on, simply cut this off with a sharp knife. Now pull off the legs and the central section of the shell by inserting your thumb under the shell where the legs were. The tail part of the shell should now pull off along with the front part of the shell. Now remove the sand tract which runs along the animal longways. It is essential to do this otherwise a completely new texture is given to the dish! Try not to break the fish up too much when doing this.

4   Now immerse in the sauce and marinate for about 2 days.

5   The traditional way of cooking this is in a tandoor on skewers but you can use an ordinary charcoal barbecue or a grill. As with any tandoori cooking, the emphasis must be on thorough cooking so it is important not to have the heat too high. One of the pitfalls of this dish is to allow the fish to dry out so try to serve it as freshly cooked as possible. You will find for quantity that about three crawfish per person is adequate but of course you can adjust this according to your generosity and pocket.

6   Serve garnished with lemon. A salad and any aubergine dish make good accompaniments.

This dish is to be found more in Pakistan than in India as of course, Hindus will not eat beef. It is very similar to roghan gosht in its preparation but as the quality of beef in India is usually inferior to that of lamb, the authentic recipe calls for a period of marination. When using a tough piece of meat, marination can last anything up to six days but with a relatively tender cut of meat the marination need only take 24 hours.

IMPERIAL/METRIC	AMERICAN
1 lb./450 g. lean beef	1 lb. lean beef
1½ teaspoons salt	1½ teaspoons salt
½ pint/3 dl. yogurt	1¼ cups yogurt
2 large onions	2 large onions
8 oz./225 g. ghee	1 cup ghee
2 oz./50 g. fresh ginger	½ cup sliced fresh ginger
4 cloves garlic	4 cloves garlic
2 teaspoons coriander powder	2 teaspoons coriander powder
1 teaspoon garam masala	1 teaspoon garam masala
½ teaspoon chilli powder	½ teaspoon chili powder
2 teaspoons paprika	2 teaspoons paprika pepper
½ teaspoon cummin seed powder	½ teaspoon cummin seed powder
2 teaspoons turmeric	2 teaspoons turmeric

1　Cut the beef into ½-inch thick slices. Then tenderise the meat which you can do either by using a mechanical tenderising machine or simply by laying the meat on your worktop and using a mallet.

2　Then rub the salt into the meat and marinate it in the yogurt for 24 hours or longer if possible.

3　With the marination complete, take a large, heavy pot and fry the onions until golden brown in the ghee. Then slice the ginger and the garlic and add to the saucepan with the rest of the spices. Stir well until you have a beautifully aromatic sauce.

4　All that remains is to add the meat along with the yogurt and cook very gently until tender. This will take from ¾ hour to 1¼ hours.

KOFTA CURRY
Curried meat balls

This dish is nearly always found at Indian parties, notably wedding feasts. This is because it is cheap to produce and it goes well with the other great 'filler-up' – rice. If you have never cooked Indian food before, this is probably the best dish to start with.

IMPERIAL/METRIC	AMERICAN
1lb./450 g. raw minced meat	1 lb. raw ground meat
1 lb./450 g. onions	1 lb. onions
6 cloves garlic	6 cloves garlic
1 oz./25 g. parsley	¾ cup chopped parsley
1 egg	1 egg
oil for deep frying	oil for deep frying
4 oz./100 g. ghee	½ cup ghee
2 teaspoons salt	2 teaspoons salt
1 teaspoon chilli powder	1 teaspoon chili powder
1 teaspoon ground black pepper	1 teaspoon ground black pepper
1 teaspoon cummin seed powder	1 teaspoon cummin seed powder
2 teaspoons garam masala	2 teaspoons garam masala
2 teaspoons paprika	2 teaspoons paprika pepper
1 teaspoon turmeric	1 teaspoon turmeric
2 oz./50 g. fresh ginger	½ cup chopped fresh ginger
½ pint/3 dl. yogurt	1¼ cups yogurt

1　Re-pass the minced meat through a mincer with half the onions, three cloves of garlic and the parsley.

2　Take the resulting mixture, add the egg and mix well with the hands. Form into 1-inch diameter balls.

3　Deep-fry the balls for 2 minutes in hot oil.

4　Slice the remaining onions and fry in the ghee until golden brown.

5　Add the spices and stir well for 10 minutes.

6　Then add the meat balls and simmer for 30 minutes turning the balls frequently to ensure that they do not stick to the bottom of the pot.

7　After 30 minutes add the yogurt and simmer for a further 30 minutes, stirring well.

Illustrated on pages 56 and 57.

BAIGAN TAMATAR
Aubergines cooked with tomatoes

With the exception of ladies' fingers (okra), baigan tamatar is probably the most popular dish available in the tandoori-style restaurants. It typifies the blandness of the northern Indian cuisine and you actually know what you are eating.

Note Always choose firm aubergines which at the height of the season should be almost black in colour. Tinned aubergines are virtually useless for this dish. The tomatoes may, however, be as ripe as you like, provided that they are still firm and the skins are not broken.

IMPERIAL/METRIC	AMERICAN
2 medium onions	2 medium onions
8 oz./225 g. ghee	1 cup ghee
1 small clove garlic	1 small clove garlic
½ teaspoon chilli powder	½ teaspoon chili powder
1 bay leaf	1 bay leaf
1-inch/2·5-cm. stick cinnamon	1-inch stick cinnamon
1½ teaspoons salt	1½ teaspoons salt
½ teaspoon ground black pepper	½ teaspoon ground black pepper
little water	little water
1 lb./450 g. tomatoes	1 lb. tomatoes
1 lb./450 g. aubergines	1 lb. eggplants
2 tablespoons tomato purée	3 tablespoons tomato paste

1 Chop the onions and fry them in the ghee until golden brown. Add the garlic, chilli powder, bay leaf, cinnamon, salt and black pepper. Also add a little water and bring to the boil, stirring constantly.

2 Now add the tomatoes, peeled and quartered, and continue to boil for 5 minutes.

3 Chop the aubergines into cubes (not forgetting to remove the tough green leaves at the bottom of the aubergine) and add to the pot with the tomato purée. Simmer for 30 minutes until the aubergines are tender but do not overcook otherwise they will disintegrate.

Illustrated on pages 56 and 57.

KEEMA PIMENTO
Minced meat with green peppers

The green pepper, is among the few exotic vegetables that are readily available at most greengrocers. However, although the green pepper's fate is usually to garnish an otherwise tired green salad, there are other uses for this delicious vegetable, and I consider the following recipe for keema pimento does it more than justice.

IMPERIAL/METRIC	AMERICAN
1 lb./450 g. green peppers	1 lb. green sweet peppers
vegetable oil	vegetable oil
1 lb./450 g. onions	1 lb. onions
2 teaspoons salt	2 teaspoons salt
2 teaspoons ground black pepper	2 teaspoons ground black pepper
½ teaspoon cummin seed powder	½ teaspoon cummin seed powder
2 teaspoons garam masala	2 teaspoons garam masala
pinch ground cinnamon	pinch ground cinnamon
1½ teaspoons chilli powder	1½ teaspoons chili powder
3 lb./1⅓ kg. raw minced meat	3 lb. raw ground meat
For garnish	
green pepper rings	green sweet pepper rings
tomatoes	tomatoes

1 Cut the green peppers into strips a ¼ inch wide, making sure that you discard all the seeds, the white centre and the green stalk. Heat the oil in a heavy pan and sauté the strips for about a minute. Then remove, transfer to a dish and place in a warm oven.

2 Now slice the onions and add to the oil. Fry until golden brown, add the salt, black pepper, cummin seed powder, garam masala, cinnamon powder and chilli powder and stir for 2 minutes.

3 Add the minced meat and cook it gently, stirring to make sure that none sticks to the bottom of the pan. This will probably take 20 minutes but it is worth cooking the minced meat well.

4 Now all that remains is to add the green peppers and again, stir over a very low heat, for a further 10 minutes.

5 Serve garnished with rings of green pepper and tomato.

Illustrated on page 32.

SEEKH KEBAB
Spicy lamb fingers

A lot of people seem to think that seekh kebab is a dish peculiar to the religious sect who wear turbans and never cut their hair. This of course is not true. The word *seekh* in Hindi means a skewer, and 'seekh kebab' is simply a kebab on a skewer. This skewer of kebab was originally cooked in the tandoor but as I explained in the case of the tandoori crawfish it is not necessary to have a five foot high conical oven to produce good tandoori crawfish or other dishes. I must confess however, that a lot of the essential flavour of the seekh kebab comes from the charcoal smoke of the fire in which it is normally cooked. The best Western compromise that I can think of for cooking this dish is a charcoal barbecue.

Note The idea behind the seekh kebab is to spice the meat but to do it in such a way that it involves no pre-cooking a spiced sauce. This is done by re-passing the minced meat through a mincer with the various spices. Another point of interest is that the skewers used in India to cook seekh kebab are different to the ones we are used to in the West. These skewers are made of iron or steel and are approximately 3 feet long and $\frac{3}{8}$ inch in diameter. It is the diameter that is significant as you can see that the meat will have a $\frac{3}{8}$-inch hole through it and in order to cook it the seekh kebab is first formed into a ball about 2 inches in diameter and then moulded into a sausage-shape on the skewers. When re-using the skewers it is essential to make sure that they are clean otherwise you will have problems removing the next set of kebabs.

IMPERIAL/METRIC	AMERICAN
1 lb./450 g. raw minced lamb	1 lb. raw ground lamb
2 medium onions	2 medium onions
2 tablespoons breadcrumbs	3 tablespoons bread crumbs
2 oz./50 g. fresh coriander	1½ cups chopped fresh coriander
½ teaspoon salt	½ teaspoon salt
1 teaspoon garam masala	1 teaspoon garam masala
1 tablespoon finely chopped green pepper	1 tablespoon finely chopped green sweet pepper
1 tablespoon lemon juice	1 tablespoon lemon juice
For garnish	
lettuce	lettuce
cucumber	cucumber

1 Re-pass the minced meat through the mincer with the onions, breadcrumbs, coriander, salt, garam masala and the green pepper.

2 Add the lemon juice to the mixture and form into balls of about 2 inches in diameter. Push these on to the skewer and gradually mould them into sausage-shapes along the metal.

3 These can either be cooked gently on a low heat with a barbecue or grill, or in the oven at 350°F., Gas Mark 4, for 15 to 20 minutes. When the meat comes off the skewer cleanly, the kebab is cooked right through and ready to serve on a bed of lettuce and cucumber.

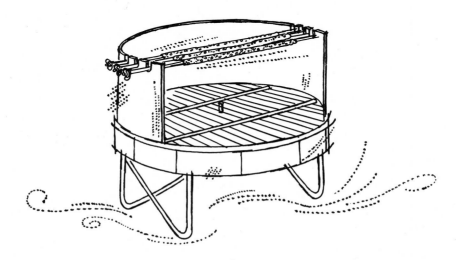

One of the delights of travelling in the Indian sub-continent is the myriad of individuals pedling their wares. It seems that in the Western world our big cities have lost the basic services that make our lives flow smoothly. In India it is still possible to find almost anything one would want to buy in the bazaars of even the largest towns. Foremost in any bazaar are the food vendors. The character of the eastern market changes entirely as dusk falls. The daily smells give way to the distinctive aroma of charcoal fires and roasting meat – the aroma of tikka kebab. There is nothing very complicated about preparing this dish, but the result is exquisite. Essentially the dish consists of marinated cubes of lean meat gently barbecued. Tikka kebab is at its best when cooked over a charcoal fire and thus is very good for an open air barbecue. However, quite reasonable results can be obtained by cooking it under a grill. The secret is in the preparation. In India goat meat is usually used but of course lamb will give perfectly acceptable results.

Note This dish is better the longer the meat is marinated. For very lean and tender meat 24 hours should be sufficient, but there is nothing wrong with leaving it for up to a week in a cool place.

IMPERIAL/METRIC	AMERICAN
1 medium onion	1 medium onion
3 tablespoons vegetable oil	scant ¼ cup vegetable oil
1 lb./450 g. lean lamb	1 lb. lean lamb
½ lemon	½ lemon
2 cloves garlic	2 cloves garlic
1 oz./25 g. fresh ginger, chopped	¼ cup chopped fresh ginger
1 teaspoon garam masala	1 teaspoon garam masala
1 teaspoon paprika	1 teaspoon paprika pepper
1 teaspoon salt	1 teaspoon salt
3 tablespoons vinegar	scant ¼ cup vinegar
½ pint/3 dl. yogurt	1¼ cups yogurt
For garnish	
onion rings	onion rings
wedges of lemon	wedges of lemon

1 Chop the onion and add to the oil.

2 Take the meat and cut into 1-inch cubes. Be sure to trim away any excess fat.

3 Take the lemon and rub all over the meat. It is best to use a shallow baking tin for this. Now rub the oil and onion mixture over the meat. It is important to get to grips with the meat and knead it well.

4 Take the remaining ingredients and liquidise together into a smooth mixture.

5 Add this mixture to the meat and blend in well. The cubes of meat should be covered by the liquid. Store in a cool place for the marination period.

6 When you come to cook the tikkas, bear in mind that they must be served and eaten when freshly cooked as they tend to dry out if left to stand. There is some skill in cooking this dish and the secret is to ensure that each cube is cooked uniformly by turning the skewer occasionally. Unlike the seekh kebab, ordinary sized skewers are used. Thread about four cubes onto each skewer and place over the charcoal or under the grill. It is better to cook slowly to ensure even cooking.

7 Serve when the outside starts to go dark brown. Tikka kebab is usually eaten with some sort of bread and I would recommend parathas as the best accompaniment Garnish with onion rings and wedges of lemon.

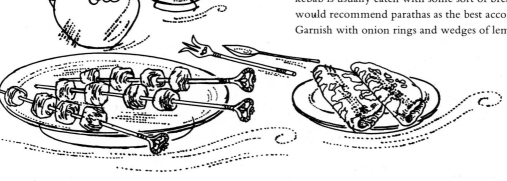

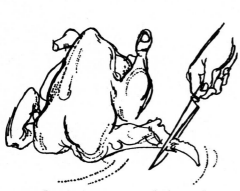

1 Before skinning the chicken, cut off the lowest joints of the wings and legs then position the bird with the breast uppermost and the cavity away from you.

2 Pinch the skin at the top of the chicken and ease away gently with a sharp knife right down to the neck end.

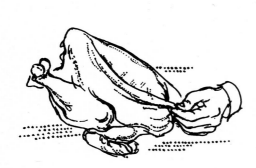

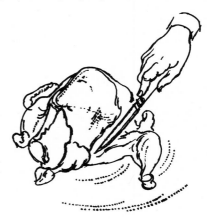

3 Turn the chicken over and continue to cut away a strip of skin from the underside of the bird. Finish by cutting off the parson's nose.

4 To joint the chicken, insert a sharp knife between the breast and leg and cut through the flesh to the thigh joint. Separate the legs from the breasts.

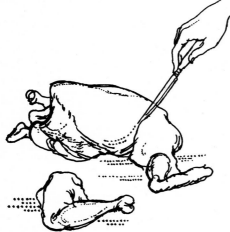

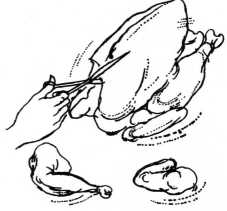

5 Remove the wing joints in the same way.

6 Divide the rest of the chicken into two halves by cutting along the breastbone and down through the backbone with scissors. Divide all the joints to make at least twelve pieces.

No Indian cookery book is complete without a recipe for that old standby, chicken curry; the following recipe may seem rather complicated at first but I assure you that it is the only way to produce something that is chicken curry and not just curried chicken. One of the advantages of this dish is that it is far better to use a cheap boiling fowl than a tender but more expensive, oven-ready fowl. Do not be put off by the fact that you can only obtain good broilers over about 4 lb. in weight, you can always use the pieces of left-overs in a biryani. Chicken curry like kofta curry, as it is quite exotic by Eastern standards and still a cheap dish to prepare, is a great favourite at wedding feasts. Of course it goes very well with rice.

IMPERIAL/METRIC	AMERICAN
1 4-lb./1¾-kg. boiling fowl	1 4-lb. stewing chicken
12 oz./350 g. ghee	1½ cups ghee
1½ lb./675 g. onions	1½ lb. onions
4 oz./100 g. fresh ginger	1 cup chopped fresh ginger
1 head garlic, about	1 head garlic, about
7 or 8 cloves	7 or 8 cloves
1 pint/6 dl. water	2½ cups water
2 teaspoons tumeric	2 teaspoons turmeric
2 teaspoons garam masala	2 teaspoons garam masala
3 teaspoons salt	3 teaspoons salt
3 teaspoons cummin seed	3 teaspoons cummin seed
powder	powder
½ teaspoon ground black	½ teaspoon ground black
pepper	pepper
1 teaspoon chilli powder	1 teaspoon chili powder
10 cardamoms	10 cardamoms
10 cloves	10 cloves
4 bay leaves	4 bay leaves
5 sticks cinnamon	5 sticks cinnamon
½ pint/3 dl. yogurt	1¼ cups yogurt

1 Those of you who have ever eaten Indian food will have noticed that all the chicken dishes use chicken which has been skinned, so the first job is to skin the fowl! There are many theories about skinning chicken but I have found that the best method is to skin the chicken virtually whole. First cut off the lowest joints of the wings and legs and lay the bird the right way up with the cavity away from you.

2 Now pinch the skin at the top of the chicken and gently cut away with a sharp knife right down to the neck end. Now turn the bird over and continue to cut away a strip of skin from the underside of the chicken, finishing by cutting off the parson's nose.

3 Next comes the jointing of the chicken, which is shown in the diagrams opposite.

4 Take a heavy, 4-pint saucepan and melt the ghee, adding half the sliced onions.

5 While they are frying on a gentle heat, liquidise the ginger, garlic and the rest of the onions with the water. When the onions are golden brown add the liquidised mixture and stir on a low heat for 10 minutes.

6 Now add the turmeric, garam masala, salt, cummin seed powder, pepper, chilli powder, cardamoms, cloves, bay leaves, and cinnamon and stir for a further 10 minutes.

7 Then add the chicken pieces and the yogurt. Cover the pan and cook on a low heat for 3 hours. You will now have beautifully cooked chicken in which the spice has permeated the meat to the bone, and the flesh will fall away at a touch when properly done.

There are many recipes for this dish, some of them complex, some very easy. The following recipe is to my mind perhaps the simplest and the most economical way of using up your left-overs. For a cook in a hurry, it gives the satisfaction of looking like a dish that has taken a lot of time to prepare when in fact it only needs about 15 minutes (assuming you have the left-over chicken curry). The recipe below is for chicken but you can adapt it to any other left-over meat. For example, lamb biryani from roghan gosht, beef biryani from pasanda.

IMPERIAL/METRIC	AMERICAN
12 oz./350 g. best Basmati rice	2 cups best Basmati rice
12 oz./350 g. left-over chicken (from chicken curry)	¾ lb. left-over chicken (from chicken curry)
½ pint/3 dl. left-over chicken curry sauce	1¼ cups left-over chicken curry sauce
½ teaspoon orange food colouring	½ teaspoon orange food coloring
For garnish	
1 hard-boiled egg	1 hard-cooked egg
2 tomatoes	2 tomatoes
1 green pepper	1 green sweet pepper

1 Cook the rice in the usual manner by boiling in twice its volume of water (see page 6). Next, drain the rice and put in a hot oven to ensure that every grain is separate.

2 Heat the curry sauce in a frying pan until it boils and then add the chicken pieces. These should be cooked over a high flame turning continuously to prevent sticking. After about 2 or 3 minutes the chicken should be well heated.

3 Now add the cooked rice along with the orange food colouring. Sauté the rice very quickly (not longer than 1 minute), until it all has an homogeneous orange colour and the chicken is well mixed in. If the rice appears too dry, add a little more curry sauce or water.

4 Transfer to a hot oval platter and garnish with the sliced, boiled egg, tomato and green pepper.

Note The perfect accompaniment to any biryani is raeta (see page 75).

Illustrated opposite.

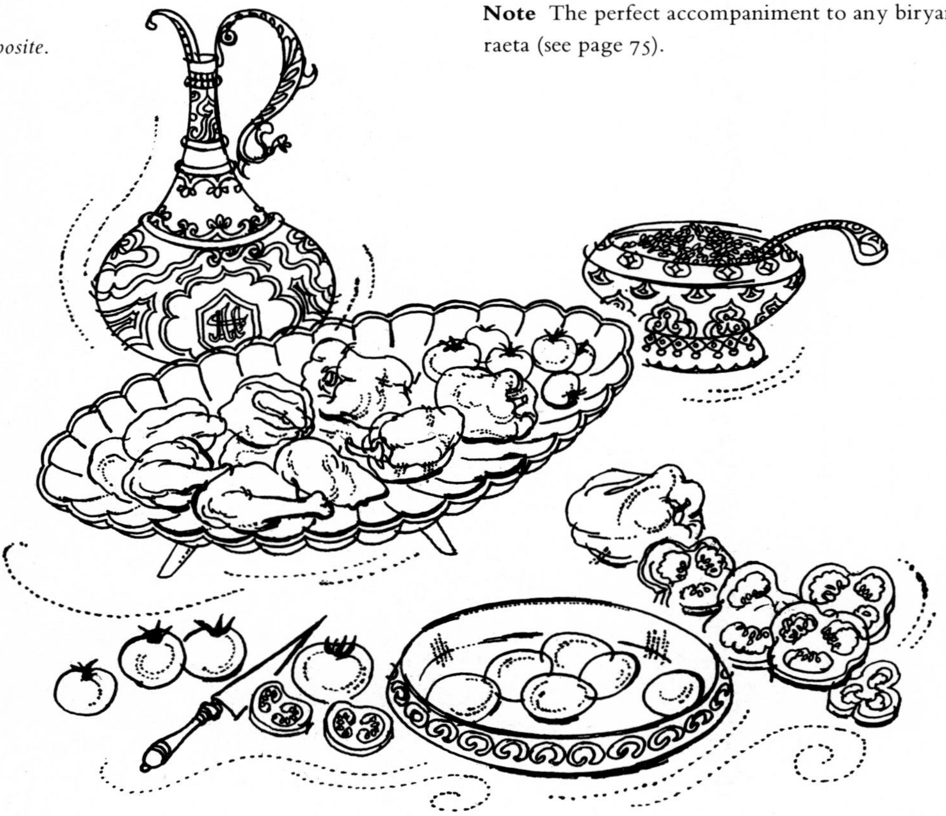

Raeta (page 75), and chicken biryani

This is without doubt the most famous of all dishes associated with northern India. Tandoori chicken owes this fame mainly to the hundreds of tandoori-style restaurants that have sprung up in the major cities of Europe in the last five years. The name 'tandoori' comes from the Hindi word *tandoor*, which means a tall, cylindrical clay oven which was used originally in north India to cook meat dishes and bread. However, it is by no means necessary to own one of these monstrous constructions in order to produce authentic tandoori chicken. As in most tandoori meat dishes, the secret lies in the preparation especially in the marinating and rubbing-in process. Those who tell you that the dish is not tandoori chicken true unless it has been cooked laboriously in a clay oven, will also tell you that the bird used must be under 12 oz. in weight. As both 12-oz. chickens and clay ovens are hard to come by in most cities, I have selected a recipe which utilises an oven-ready frozen chicken and a conventional stove.

IMPERIAL/METRIC	AMERICAN
1 3-lb./1⅓-kg. oven-ready chicken	1 3-lb. oven-ready chicken
¼ pint/1½ dl. vinegar	⅔ cup vinegar
1 pint/6 dl. yogurt	2½ cups yogurt
2 large onions	2 large onions
4 cloves garlic	4 cloves garlic
2 oz./50 g. fresh ginger, unpeeled	½ cup unpeeled fresh ginger
1 lemon	1 lemon
2 teaspoons garam masala	2 teaspoons garam masala
1 teaspoon chilli powder	1 teaspoon chili powder
1 teaspoon paprika	1 teaspoon paprika pepper
½ teaspoon yellow food colouring	½ teaspoon yellow food coloring
1½ teaspoons salt	1½ teaspoons salt
For garnish	
lettuce	lettuce
tomatoes	tomatoes
onion rings	onion rings

Illustrated on pages 24 and 25.

1 Skin and quarter the chicken and make two ½-inch deep cuts in each of the quarters. It is essential not to go too deep otherwise the chicken will break up during cooking.

2 Place the vinegar and a little of the yogurt in a liquidiser, switch the liquidiser on to its lowest speed and add pieces of onion, garlic, and peeled ginger sparingly, so that the liquidiser is not overloaded.

3 Now quarter the lemon and add three quarters to the liquidiser; liquidise until a smooth sauce is obtained. Pour off a little of this liquid into a bowl and add the rest of the spices except the salt, mixing well to ensure that there are no lumps.

4 Return the sauce to the liquidiser and liquidise for another 30 seconds.

5 Now take the chicken quarters and rub well with the salt and the remaining quarter of lemon, ensuring that the juice gets right inside the cuts that you made earlier. This rubbing-in process makes it easier for the sauce to penetrate during the marinating process. Lay the chicken pieces in a shallow baking tray, add the marinade and place in a fridge for 24 to 48 hours. It is advisable to cover the tray with baking foil to ensure that the smells of the fridge do not penetrate the chicken and vice-versa.

6 Remove the baking foil after the 2 days and transfer the baking tray to an oven at 350°F., Gas Mark 4. Cook for 1½ hours.

7 Remove the chicken from the liquid and serve the yogurt mixture separately if liked.
Tandoori chicken is best served on a bed of lettuce leaves and garnished with tomatoes and onion rings.

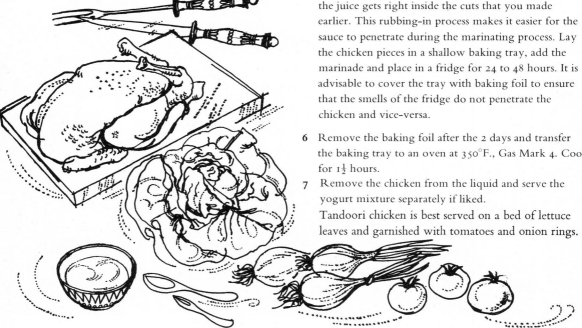

In every busy market place in northern India and Pakistan you will find a pakora wallah. I have heard the pakora described in many ways, perhaps the most apt being that it is like a spiced Yorkshire pudding with a filling. Some may say this is an unfair judgment on the pakora, as the Yorkshire pudding is not done justice by the cheap purveyors in this country but quite the reverse is true in India where the roadside vendors have perfected the art of pakora-making to such a degree that you always find queues of people by the stalls waiting to crunch their way through a $\frac{1}{4}$ lb. of their favourite pakora. Pakoras may be made of many things, but of course the most essential thing is the batter.

Note You can fill pakoras with almost any vegetable or fruit but the ones that I have found the most tasty and which are well received by most people are the ones made from thin slices of aubergine (baigan pakora), and those made from spinach (saag pakora). To make the former, the aubergines should be sliced to an $\frac{1}{8}$-inch thickness. The rounds of the aubergine are then dipped into the batter and deep-fried in clean cooking oil. If it is too hot you will find that the pakoras go very dark brown on the outside and stay soft and stodgy inside; if the oil is too cool they will be laden with fat when taken out. If in doubt, follow the manufacturer's recommended temperature for fritters. When using spinach or any other sort of leaf, it is essential to ensure that the leaves are dry, otherwise the frying oil will deteriorate very quickly. You will find pakoras an interesting and simple snack to serve at teatime and they make a change from biscuits and cucumber sandwiches!

IMPERIAL/METRIC	AMERICAN
1 medium onion	1 medium onion
$\frac{1}{4}$ lemon	$\frac{1}{4}$ lemon
$\frac{1}{2}$ pint/3 dl. yogurt	1$\frac{1}{4}$ cups yogurt
1 teaspoon chilli powder	1 teaspoon chili powder
$\frac{1}{2}$ teaspoon dry mustard	$\frac{1}{2}$ teaspoon dry mustard
5–6 oz./150–175 g. gram flour or chick-pea flour	1$\frac{1}{4}$–1$\frac{1}{2}$ cups gram flour or chick-pea flour
vegetable oil	vegetable oil

Illustrated on page 28.

1 Cut up the onion and lemon into small pieces and add it with the yogurt to a liquidiser and bring to a smooth sauce. Pour this out into a large mixing bowl and add the chilli powder and mustard.

2 Now comes the most important part of the batter-making, the addition of the gram flour. Those of you who are not familiar with this will realise on opening the packet that it is much finer than our ordinary flour. Because of this, it forms lumps a lot more easily, and it is a lot more difficult to mix into the batter. It is essential then that the gram flour be well sieved into the mixture and it should be stirred constantly, preferably with a wire whisk. Keep adding the flour until you have obtained a batter which forms small peaks which disintegrate 15 or 20 seconds after they have formed. Depending on how liquid the yogurt is, you may have to add more or less gram flour. You should find that this batter will keep for weeks if it is covered and placed in a fridge and that it is also quite easy to freeze – very useful if you ever want teatime snacks in a hurry.

Plain boiled rice (page 6), and tarka dal (page 30)

Ladies' fingers (page 22), and tomato salad

BHINDI BHAJI
Ladies' fingers

Bhindi, ladies' fingers, okra, call it what you will, this is the vegetable that everybody associates with Indian cooking. I think it is true to say that this vegetable is found nowhere outside the sub-continent and certainly no-one I have met has failed to express their appreciation of this dish when properly cooked. However, as with all popular dishes there are good and bad concoctions served under the guise of bhindi bhaji. Those to be shunned when eating in an Indian restaurant are the dishes that come with the bhindi whole in a long, stringy form. These dishes have undoubtedly been made from canned bhindi, and canning, in my opinion, has never successfully preserved the bhindi's essential flavour. You can be sure, then, that if the bhindi comes in a chopped form it is fresh, but also beware of the concoctions that boast a lot of sauce. This proves that it has been made by a chef who does not really understand what he should be doing and that the essence of cooking bhindi is that you should taste the vegetable and not anything else. The bhindi should be immediately recognisable as such. Now that you know what you are trying to achieve I am sure you will be able to tackle this recipe with confidence!

IMPERIAL/METRIC	AMERICAN
2 large onions	2 large onions
6 oz./175 g. ghee	$\frac{3}{4}$ cup ghee
4 cloves garlic	4 cloves garlic
pinch black pepper	pinch black pepper
pinch salt	pinch salt
2 teaspoons coriander powder	2 teaspoons coriander powder
$\frac{1}{2}$ teaspoon tumeric	$\frac{1}{2}$ teaspoon turmeric
1 lb./450 g. fresh bhindi	1 lb. fresh bhindi
4 oz./100 g. canned tomatoes	$\frac{1}{2}$ cup canned tomatoes
1 teaspoon fresh chopped mint	1 teaspoon fresh chopped mint
$\frac{1}{2}$ teaspoon garam masala	$\frac{1}{2}$ teaspoon garam masala

For garnish

fresh mint	fresh mint

Illustrated on page 21.

1 Slice one onion and fry in the ghee in a heavy pot.

2 Liquidise the remaining onion and the garlic along with the black pepper, salt, coriander and turmeric.

3 Add this mixture to the onions and cook on a medium heat for 5 minutes.

4 Meanwhile, prepare the bhindi. To do this it is essential to wash it thoroughly – remember it has come all the way from India and you do not know what it might have picked up on the way! Having done this, it is necessary to top and tail each of the ladies' fingers and chop them into $\frac{1}{2}$-inch pieces.

5 Now add these to the spices. It is imperative that you stir the bhindi pieces and take care not to crush or mash them in any way. Cover the pot with a lid and cook on a very low flame for about 20 minutes.

6 Then add the canned tomatoes, the mint and the garam masala. The bhindi will be quite soft by now so it is even more important to be careful when stirring in these ingredients. Simmer for 15 minutes.

7 Serve garnished with fresh mint.

SAAG ALOO
Curried spinach

Most Western people with the exception of the Americans, have an aversion to spinach. Whilst they will agree that it is good for the constitution, they will usually on no account touch it themselves. This is a great shame because, like cabbage, spinach when properly cooked is a very tasty vegetable. Saag aloo is one of the few dishes which really brings out the fresh taste of spinach. If you can bring yourself to throw tradition to the winds I am sure that you will find it is a very worthwhile dish.

IMPERIAL/METRIC	AMERICAN
2 large onions	2 large onions
4 oz./100 g. ghee	½ cup ghee
½ teaspoon coriander seeds	½ teaspoon coriander seeds
½ teaspoon cummin seeds	½ teaspoon cummin seeds
½ teaspoon chilli powder	½ teaspoon chili powder
½ teaspoon coriander powder	½ teaspoon coriander powder
2 lb./900 g. fresh spinach or 1 lb./450 g. frozen spinach	2 lb. fresh spinach or 1 lb. frozen spinach
1 lb./450 g. potatoes	1 lb. potatoes
½ teaspoon salt	½ teaspoon salt
2 teaspoons fenugreek	2 teaspoons fenugreek
2 green chillis (optional)	2 green chilis (optional)
4 oz./100 g. canned tomatoes	½ cup canned tomatoes
2 oz./50 g. fresh ginger	½ cup thinly sliced fresh ginger

1 Slice 1 onion and fry in the ghee in a heavy saucepan until golden brown. Then add the coriander and cummin seeds and cook for a minute.

2 Meanwhile, liquidise the rest of the onions and the chilli powder together with the coriander powder. Stir the liquid into the onions. Cook for 5 minutes.

3 Wash the spinach and chop it into small pieces. Cook this for 10 minutes until it is tender.

4 This gives you time to chop and peel the potatoes, cutting into 1-inch cubes and then parboil for 5 to 8 minutes in slightly salted water.

5 Drain the water off the potatoes and add, with the spinach, salt, fenugreek and chillis, to the main pot. Stir in well and cook on a very low heat for approximately 10 minutes, turning occasionally.

6 Then add the tomatoes and thinly sliced ginger. Cover and simmer for 10 minutes. Saag aloo is one of the few Indian dishes that does deteriorate on keeping so it is always best freshly made and served as soon as possible.

Parathas (page 27), tandoori chicken (page 18), and poppadums (page 6)

Chapattys need no introduction from me except to say that a well made chapatty is a joy to eat. As in rice cooking the secret of the chapatty does not lie so much in the cooking as in the basic ingredients. A lot of the major cities nowadays have Indian delicatessens and even one or two of the larger milling firms make their own special brand of flour, known as chapatty flour or *ata*. It is this type of flour that you should be looking for to make chapattys. It is a mistake to make chapattys with wholemeal flour as I have tried and the result is far too starchy. The following quantities will make enough for four people.

Note In India they usually cook chapattys on a hemispherical iron plate placed over the heat source called a *tawa*, but of course these are not always available in the West and so you can make a compromise by using perhaps an upturned frying pan or a griddle. Chapattys should always be eaten fresh as a re-warmed chapatty is like leather. This fact is worth bearing in mind when you have guests and are trying to decide whether to have rice or some form of bread; the rice will release you for your guests whereas you will have to cook right up to the last minute if you choose one of the breads.

IMPERIAL/METRIC	AMERICAN
8 oz./225 g. chapatty flour	2 cups chapatty flour
some water	some water
$\frac{1}{2}$ teaspoon salt	$\frac{1}{2}$ teaspoon salt

1 Add the salt to the chapatty flour and gradually add the water until you obtain an homogeneous dough which is wet to the touch. The dough, however, should be quite firm and hard.

2 To make one chapatty break off a piece of the dough approximately 2 inches in diameter and roll in some dry flour. Place the ball on a floured board and roll into a disc approximately 6 inches in diameter. The chapatty should be about $\frac{1}{8}$ inch thick.

3 Flour the tawa or equivalent lightly. It should be so hot that when water is thrown on it, it spatters immediately. Take the chapatty and lay it over the top of the tawa for 45 seconds and then turn it and cook for a further 45 seconds.

4 Now take the chapatty and move the tawa to one side and place the chapatty on the naked heat source if electric or under the grill of an electric or gas cooker. You will see that the chapatty will swell out and that you get one or two small burnt patches. Needless to say, these should not be too large.

5 Serve at the table wrapped in a warm cloth.

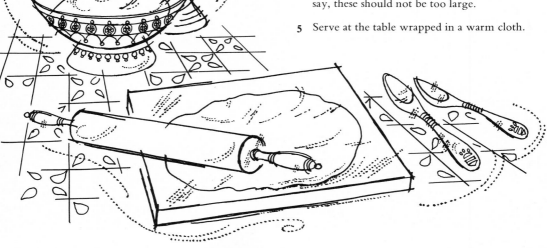

PARATHAS
Fried bread

This is another of the breads held favourite by most Westerners. It is perhaps more simple to make than ordinary chapatty as its cooking technique is similar to Western customs. The paratha is slightly larger in diameter and about twice as thick as the chapatty therefore the preceding ingredients will make half the number of parathas. Do not forget of course that the bread will be twice as filling.

IMPERIAL/METRIC	AMERICAN
8 oz./225 g. chapatty flour	2 cups chapatty flour
pinch salt	pinch salt
some water	some water
4 oz./100 g. ghee	$\frac{1}{2}$ cup ghee

Illustrated on page 24.

1 Take a 4-inch ball of dough, coat in flour and roll it out as thinly as possible on a floured board.

2 Now take the melted ghee, and with a pastry brush paint the liquid fat all over the upper surface of the dough. Now fold the paratha and reform into a round ball. Roll this out to a disc 6 inches wide and $\frac{1}{4}$–$\frac{1}{2}$ inch thick.

3 Pour a little of the melted ghee into the hot frying pan and fry the paratha on both sides until it is crisp on the outside. Serve hot.

PURI
Deep-fried bread

Puri is in essence a deep-fried chapatty with the addition of ghee in the dough. Puris are traditionally served at breakfast with coffee, but they are equally apt at an evening meal. Eight ounces of chapatty flour will make approximately twelve puris as they are thinner than chapattys.

IMPERIAL/METRIC	AMERICAN
4 oz./100 g. ghee	$\frac{1}{2}$ cup ghee
8 oz./225 g. chapatty flour	2 cups chapatty flour
some water	some water
vegetable oil	vegetable oil

1 Rub the ghee into the flour and then make a chapatty-like dough by adding water.

2 Break off 1-inch pieces and roll out to 5-inch discs.

3 Heat the oil and drop in the puri carefully to avoid creasing it. If the oil is the right temperature the puri will immediately puff up into a ball and float to the surface. When it does this you should push it underneath until it is crisp on both sides.

4 Lift it out, drain off excess oil and store in a warm dish.

Chaat (page 72), and pakoras (page 19)

Aviyal (page 36), and stuffed halibut (page 43)

Dal is, if you like, the real Indian food, in as much as a very large percentage of the five hundred millions of Indians eat dal every day as a part of their staple diet. It is in essence very simple in its preparation but I feel that a book on Indian cookery would not be complete without the inclusion of at least one form of dal. In Great Britain most people are only familiar with lentils whilst in America chick-peas are well-known, but in addition to these two there are a whole range of grams and pulses which the Indians make into a delicious, thick soup-like sauce to accompany their otherwise plain rice. The following recipe makes use of the ordinary, easily available, red split lentils.

IMPERIAL/METRIC	AMERICAN
1 lb./450 g. lentils	1 lb. lentils
2 pints/generous litre water	2½ pints water
1 teaspoon salt	1 teaspoon salt
1 teaspoon turmeric	1 teaspoon turmeric
1 medium onion	1 medium onion
3 cloves garlic	3 cloves garlic
2 chillis	2 chilis
For garnish	
garlic	garlic
½ teaspoon cummin seeds	½ teaspoon cummin seeds
little vegetable oil	little vegetable oil

Illustrated on page 20.

1 As with rice, it is essential to wash the dal as you never know what you may find. The best way to wash any type of grain is to put it in a large pot and run the cold tap on it continuously while you stir it. Even when you have done this keep an eagle eye on it for the odd small stone that may have settled and not been washed away.

2 Take the dal and place in a saucepan covered by 2 pints of water. Bring the water to the boil and add the salt, turmeric and onion and 2 cloves of the garlic along with the 2 whole chillis. Cover with the lid and simmer for approximately 20 minutes until cooked. When cooked the dal should be yellow in colour and have the consistency of sloppy porridge.

3 The secret of tarka dal lies in the serving. It should be served piping hot garnished with cummin seeds and slices of garlic quick-fried and poured over the dal.

KULFI MALAI
Mango ice cream

In general Indian sweets are not well known in the West, especially the more difficult ones, as Indian restaurants are usually incapable of making them to a good standard. Kulfi malai is one of these sweets. Much has been made of the French and Italian ice creams, but in my opinion this mango ice cream is the most exquisite I have ever had. Although some of the ingredients are a little difficult to obtain it is in fact quite simple to make.

Note In India this dish is always garnished with very finely beaten silver foil, known as *varak*. It is well worth the extra expense if you can get hold of this silver.

IMPERIAL/METRIC	AMERICAN
12-oz./350-g. can condensed milk	12-oz. can condensed milk
½ pint/3 dl. double cream	1¼ cups double cream
4 oz./100 g. granulated sugar	½ cup granulated sugar
1 tablespoon grated almonds	1 tablespoon grated almonds
1 tablespoon grated pistachios	1 tablespoon grated pistachios
12-oz./350-g. can mango slices or pulp	12-oz. can mango slices or pulp
1 tablespoon kewra water	1 tablespoon kewra water
For garnish	
finely beaten silver foil	finely beaten silver foil

1 Boil the milk and the cream together with the sugar stirring constantly and leave to simmer on a very low flame for 30 minutes.

2 Then add the almonds and pistachios, stirring in well and cool to room temperature by standing the saucepan in running cold water.

3 Now add the mango pulp or crushed slices. If using the latter it is necessary to drain off half the juice from the can. Also add the kewra water.

4 Mix the preparation well with a wire whisk and place to set in moulds. These may be any shape you like, but traditionally the kulfi wallahs of India use conical aluminium moulds with screw tops.

5 Place the moulds in the freezer and the kulfi will be ready when solid. As this recipe contains no artificial gelling agents you will find that on removal from the freezer it will melt very quickly. It is therefore necessary to keep the moulds in the fridge until serving.

Illustrated on page 61.

CONCLUSION ON NORTH INDIA

Liquid dishes like roghan gosht, kofta curry, chicken curry and keema pimento are usually taken with rice whilst the dry ones like tandoori chicken and seekh kebab are traditionally accompanied by bread only. As I have said in the Introduction, it is best not to have bread and rice together but obviously there is no harm in trying one of the breads in small quantities along with some rice. Suitable accompaniments to most of the dishes are bhindi, baigan tamatar and lashings of raeta (see Chapter 5). Chicken biryani is very nice on its own with perhaps just a little raeta. To finish up with, the kulfi malai is probably the best thing I know to cool fire-struck guests!

Minced meat with green peppers (page 11), and stuffed aubergines (page 35)

SOUTH INDIA

Traditionally, southern India has been the home of the hot curry. But it would be unfair to judge the food of this region purely on the fiery concoctions that emanate from the region around Madras, as there are numerous other tasty dishes to be found in this area. Perhaps the most exotic of these comes from the Malabar coast off Kerala. The people of the south, being Hindus do not usually eat much meat and therefore most of the main dishes from southern India centre around vegetables. Any meat dishes you find in this chapter will be either Muslim dishes or dishes prepared by the Syrian Christians who have inhabited a lot of the south and west coast. Most of the recipes in this chapter are dedicated to those of you who like your curries hot, but I must add by way of warning that you can not only burn your palate by excessive addition of hot spices, but also upset your stomach. So please do not be tempted to 'hot up' a dish unless you are absolutely sure of your culinary skill.

GOODHI BHAJI

Marrows are a vegetable freely available in most Western countries and which most people with a vegetable garden and sufficient time find very easy to grow. This recipe, a typically vegetarian one, makes use of only young marrows which should never be more than about six or seven inches in length. I must confess that whenever I have tasted marrows cooked in a Western style, they always seem rather insipid to me, but having tasted the Indian method of cooking them, I consider that Indian cooks have hit upon a method of spicing which brings out the true flavour of the marrow.

IMPERIAL/METRIC	AMERICAN
2 lb./900 g. young marrows	2 lb. squash
vegetable oil	vegetable oil
1½ teaspoons mustard seeds	1½ teaspoons mustard seeds
2 medium onions	2 medium onions
2 tomatoes	2 tomatoes
1½ teaspoons garam masala	1½ teaspoons garam masala
½ teaspoon turmeric	½ teaspoon turmeric
1 teaspoon chilli powder	1 teaspoon chili powder
1 teaspoon ground black pepper	1 teaspoon ground black pepper
½ teaspoon salt	½ teaspoon salt
3 oz./75 g. desiccated coconut	1 cup shredded coconut
For garnish	
wedges of lemon	wedges of lemon

1 To prepare the marrow, first peel it then cut it lengthways and scoop out all the seeds. Next dice into 1-inch cubes.

2 Heat a little of the vegetable oil until smoking and then add the mustard seeds and fry until they begin to splutter. Now add a little more of the vegetable oil and the sliced onions. Fry until golden brown.

3 Slice the tomatoes and add to the pot together with the garam masala, turmeric, chilli powder, and black pepper, and fry gently on a low heat for 5 or 6 minutes.

4 Meanwhile, rub marrow with the salt and the desiccated coconut. Now add to pot and simmer with the pot covered for about 15 minutes.

5 Serve with wedges of lemon.

No section on south India would be complete without a recipe for mulligatawny soup. Mulligatawny is a tamil word and literally translated it means chilli water, but with the advent of the British Raj in India the name took on a completely different meaning. Prior to this, Indian food knew no soup as such and it was only the demand from the British army officers for a traditional appetiser to start their Indian meals that mulligatawny soup came about. Since the Raj there have been many different methods of preparing mulligatawny and the following recipe is the basic one. It demands the use of meat stock but it can be made from any meat stock cube reconstituted according to the directions. This may sound a little unauthentic but it must be borne in mind that mulligatawny is in itself a peculiar un-Indian dish and thus anything goes!

IMPERIAL/METRIC	AMERICAN
1 large onion	1 large onion
1 clove garlic	1 clove garlic
1 teaspoon ground ginger	1 teaspoon ground ginger
2 green chillis	2 green chilis
2 oz./50 g. ghee	scant $\frac{1}{4}$ cup ghee
$\frac{1}{2}$ teaspoon coriander powder	$\frac{1}{2}$ teaspoon coriander powder
$\frac{1}{2}$ teaspoon turmeric	$\frac{1}{2}$ teaspoon turmeric
$\frac{1}{2}$ teaspoon cummin seed	$\frac{1}{2}$ teaspoon cummin seed
1 teaspoon salt	1 teaspoon salt
$\frac{1}{2}$ teaspoon fenugreek powder	$\frac{1}{2}$ teaspoon fenugreek powder
2 pints/$1\frac{1}{4}$ litres meat stock	$2\frac{1}{2}$ pints meat stock

1 Peel and slice the onion with the garlic. Fry with the ground ginger and chillis in the ghee for 2 minutes.

2 Then add the coriander, turmeric, cummin seed, salt and fenugreek powder. Cook for about 3 minutes.

3 Finally add the stock and bring to the boil. Simmer gently for 10 minutes and serve.

ONION PAKORA

Onion pakoras are one of the most popular hors d'oeuvres or starters in the average Indian restaurant. Whilst I cannot concede that they can ever match up to either baigan or saag pakora (see Chapter 1), I must confess that they have a certain flavour about them that is unmistakably eastern. They are very simple to make using the pakora recipe given in the previous chapter but there is something to be said for using the recipe which I give for preparing the onion before use.

IMPERIAL/METRIC	AMERICAN
1 pint/6 dl. yogurt	$2\frac{1}{2}$ cups yogurt
1 tablespoon chopped fresh ginger	1 tablespoon chopped fresh ginger
1 clove garlic	1 clove garlic
1 teaspoon chilli powder	1 teaspoon chili powder
$\frac{1}{2}$ lemon	$\frac{1}{2}$ lemon
1 teaspoon salt	1 teaspoon salt
2 large onions	2 large onions
vegetable oil	vegetable oil

1 Place all the ingredients with the exception of the onion and oil in a liquidiser and liquidise to a thin pulp. Remove and place to one side.

2 Peel the onions and cut crossways to form onion rings. Add the discarded parts of the onion to the mixture and re-liquidise. Marinate the onion rings in the mixture overnight.

3 To cook, dip each ring into the pakora batter and fry individually in medium deep fat. You will find this method imparts far more flavour to the otherwise conventional onion pakora.

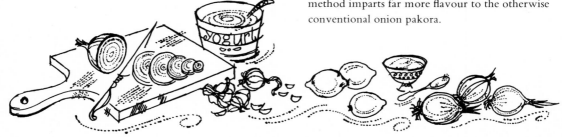

Nearly every country in the world that has a cuisine of its own seems to have a dish involving stuffed aubergines. India is no exception to this and the following recipe is rather peculiar for an Indian dish in that it makes use of the technique of roasting, a practice that is not always easy in India and Pakistan due to the lack of suitable ovens. This dish can also be fried but baking retains a lot of the original flavour of the aubergines and thus is to be considered a superior method.

If you have ever shopped for aubergines you will find that they vary a great deal in size and shape. The most readily available are the long variety; these are most suitable for making thin slices for pakoras (see Chapter 1). However, they also come in shorter, squat shapes which are the type you need for this dish.

IMPERIAL/METRIC	AMERICAN
4 aubergines (round variety)	4 eggplants (round variety)
1 teaspoon salt	1 teaspoon salt
$\frac{1}{2}$ teaspoon white pepper	$\frac{1}{2}$ teaspoon white pepper
1 large onion	1 large onion
4 oz./100 g. ghee	$\frac{1}{2}$ cup ghee
4 oz./100 g. peas	$\frac{3}{4}$ cup peas
4 oz./100 g. carrots	$\frac{1}{4}$ cup carrots
8 oz./225 g. tomatoes	$\frac{1}{2}$ lb. tomatoes
$\frac{1}{2}$ teaspoon paprika	$\frac{1}{2}$ teaspoon paprika pepper
1 teaspoon finely chopped ginger	1 teaspoon finely chopped ginger
For garnish	
mint or parsley	mint or parsley

Illustrated on page 32.

1 Wash the aubergines and remove the thick leafy sepals at the top of each one. Boil in slightly salted water for about 10 minutes. They should now be half-cooked.

2 Cut each one into halves and scoop out the pulp leaving approximately $\frac{1}{2}$ inch all the way around. Now season the cases with a pinch of the salt and the white pepper.

3 In a heavy frying pan fry the chopped onions lightly in the ghee. Then add the peas (these may be fresh, dried, or frozen but not canned), and the washed and diced carrots. Alternatively, one can use canned carrots but ensure that these are well drained before adding to the pan.

4 Now take the aubergine pulp and chop it and also add this to the frying pan with the peeled and chopped tomatoes. Cook gently until all the vegetables are cooked.

5 Now add the paprika, the rest of the salt and the finely chopped ginger. Again, half the quantity of ground ginger would perhaps be easier, even if it does not impart quite the same intensity of flavour. Stir for 2 minutes.

6 Arrange the aubergine halves in a baking tray and fill each case with the fried pulp. Now place the tray in an oven at 350°F., Gas Mark 4, and bake for approximately 20 minutes, until golden brown.

7 Serve garnished with mint or parsley.

Aviyal is the name given to any southern Indian vegetable dish which includes a mixture of many vegetables and seeds. Southern India abounds in exotic fruits, seeds and vegetables like jackfruit, drumsticks, bitter gourds, green coconut and mango, all of which are very difficult to obtain in the West, unless canned which is useless for good vegetable cooking. The following recipe utilises only those freely available vegetables such as carrots, broccoli and green beans. Once you have gained experience in your Indian cooking, you will, I think, be able to use this recipe as the basis for making many vegetable dishes, as you will see that the idea as I have stressed before, is to spice the vegetable without losing its flavour. So, after making this one, try adding different vegetables – the only things you must be sure of are that they are cooked, and that you do not mask the flavour.

IMPERIAL/METRIC	AMERICAN
8 oz./225 g. desiccated coconut	2⅔ cups shredded coconut
½ pint/3 dl. water	1¼ cups water
4 oz./100 g. ghee	½ cup ghee
1 oz./25 g. fresh ginger	1½ tablespoons chopped fresh ginger
3 cloves garlic	3 cloves garlic
½ teaspoon mustard seeds	½ teaspoon mustard seeds
1 large onion	1 large onion
2 teaspoons coriander powder	2 teaspoons coriander powder
3 teaspoons garam masala	3 teaspoons garam masala
1 teaspoon turmeric	1 teaspoon turmeric
2 teaspoons salt	2 teaspoons salt
8 oz./225 g. broccoli or kale	½ lb. broccoli or kale
2 green peppers	2 green sweet peppers
6 oz./175 g. carrots	⅓ lb. carrots
4 oz./100 g. runner beans	¼ lb. runner beans
1 green chilli	1 green chili
For garnish	
4 oz./100 g. fresh coriander	2⅔ cups chopped fresh coriander

1 Liquidise the coconut and water together to produce a smooth pureé.

2 Heat the ghee in a heavy saucepan and add the chopped ginger, garlic, and mustard seeds and fry for about a minute. Then add the onion and fry until golden brown, being careful not to burn.

3 Add the coriander powder, garam masala, turmeric and salt and simmer for about 5 minutes.

4 Meanwhile, take the vegetables and wash them and chop into 1-inch pieces; with the green peppers be sure to remove the white pith and the seeds. Now add them to the pot and stir in well. Turn them over for about 5 minutes and then add the coconut purée and the green chilli and bring the whole mixture to the boil and simmer for about 15 minutes with the pot covered.

5 Serve sprinkled with the chopped coriander.

Illustrated on page 29.

Ask any southern Indian for a vegetable dish typical of his area and he will immediately say: 'Bhagare baigan'. This dish is another proof of how vegetarian cooks can make the same vegetable taste completely different but still allow it to retain its original fresh taste. Bhagare baigan makes use of the sourness of tamarind to offset the sweetish taste of the aubergine.

IMPERIAL/METRIC	AMERICAN
1½ lb./625 g. aubergines (round variety)	1½ lb. eggplants (round variety)
vegetable oil	vegetable oil
2 large onions	2 large onions
1 teaspoon mustard seeds	1 teaspoon mustard seeds
4 oz./100 g. ghee	½ cup ghee
1½ teaspoons coriander powder	1½ teaspoons coriander powder
1 green chilli	1 green chili
½ teaspoon chilli powder	½ teaspoon chili powder
1 tablespoon desiccated coconut	1 tablespoon shredded coconut
3 cloves garlic	3 cloves garlic
1 teaspoon turmeric	1 teaspoon turmeric
1 teaspoon garam masala	1 teaspoon garam masala
4 oz./100 g. tamarind	4 oz. tamarind
1 teaspoon sugar	1 teaspoon sugar
3 bay leaves	3 bay leaves

1 Wash and trim the aubergines and cut into quarters. Heat some vegetable oil or mustard oil in a heavy frying pan and sauté the aubergine quarters until the skins just begin to turn crisp and brown. Remove from the pan and put on one side.

2 Now take a large saucepan and fry the sliced onions and mustard seeds in the ghee until golden brown, then add the coriander and the chilli. Cook for 5 minutes. Then add the chilli powder, coconut, garlic and turmeric, along with the garam masala and fry for a further 3 minutes.

3 Meanwhile, soak the tamarind in a little hot water and after about 10 minutes squeeze this out and add the water, together with the sugar. Stir in well and add the aubergines. Cover and cook for 10 to 15 minutes until the aubergines are tender, turning occasionally. As with the bhindi bhaji it is essential to make sure that you are not too rough when stirring the pot otherwise you will crush the aubergines and this will mar the appearance of the dish when it is served.

4 Now fry the bay leaves in a little oil, and pour onto the top of the dish just before serving.

Dosas are the southern Indian equivalent of a pancake. However, they are made in a slightly different way, using whole rice and urhad dal instead of the plain flour used in Western style pancakes. They are usually made very thin and filled with a dry vegetable mixture and served rolled up and sprinkled with paprika and lemon juice. In southern India they are often taken for breakfast with coffee. Following the basic recipe for the dosa you will see a recipe for a potato-based filling. This is just one of the many fillings that one can use and any dry vegetable or meat dish will be found quite acceptable as a filling.

IMPERIAL/METRIC	AMERICAN
2 oz./50 g. rice	4 tablespoons rice
6 oz./175 g. urhard dal	$\frac{3}{4}$ cup urhard dal
pinch bicarbonate soda	pinch baking soda
1 teaspoon chilli powder	1 teaspoon chili powder
vegetable oil	vegetable oil

1 Wash the rice and dal well and soak overnight in approximately 1 pint of water. Grind in a liquidiser to the consistency of condensed milk.

2 Beat in the bicarbonate of soda and the chilli powder and allow to stand for 15 minutes.

3 Using a heavy frying pan fry like conventional pancakes ensuring that the vegetable oil is very hot.

4 When cooked remove and store on a warm plate until ready for the filling.

Dosa Filling

IMPERIAL/METRIC	AMERICAN
2 lb./1 kg. potatoes	2 lb. potatoes
4 tablespoons vegetable oil	$\frac{1}{3}$ cup vegetable oil
2 teaspoons mustard seeds	2 teaspoons mustard seeds
6 curry leaves	6 curry leaves
1 teaspoon salt	1 teaspoon salt
$\frac{1}{2}$ teaspoon turmeric	$\frac{1}{2}$ teaspoon turmeric
$\frac{1}{2}$ teaspoon chilli powder	$\frac{1}{2}$ teaspoon chili powder
2 large onions	2 large onions
8 oz./225 g. tomatoes	$\frac{1}{2}$ lb. tomatoes
$\frac{1}{4}$ pint/1$\frac{1}{2}$ dl. water	$\frac{2}{3}$ cup water

For garnish

wedges of lemon	wedges of lemon
paprika	paprika pepper

1 Peel and chop the potatoes into 1-inch cubes.

2 Now take a heavy saucepan and heat the vegetable oil until it is almost smoking. Add the mustard seeds and when they begin to burst quickly cover the pan to prevent the seeds from popping everywhere.

3 Add the crushed curry leaves (these are available in most Indian delicatessens), salt and turmeric, and the chilli powder and stir for 2 minutes.

4 Now add the potatoes and fry gently for a minute.

5 Peel and slice the onions and add the tomatoes and approximately $\frac{1}{4}$ pint of water and simmer for 10 minutes until the potatoes are soft. If necessary, evaporate any excess liquid to produce a dry mixture.

6 Take this mixture and fill each pancake with it. Serve garnished with wedges of lemon and sprinkled with paprika.

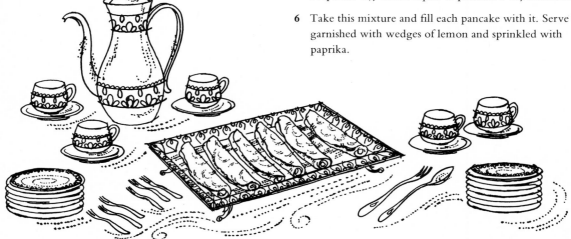

There is nothing peculiar to southern India about samosa as they are eaten throughout the sub-continent. They are, if you like, the Indian equivalent of the Cornish pasty, being originally designed as a convenient way of carrying meat and in some cases, a sweet dish, for the midday meal. Bearing this in mind then, it would be pointless for me to give you recipes for all the fillings with which samosas can be made, and so I will merely give you the recipe for the pastry which is the essential part. The most popular samosa in India is the one with a simply prepared filling of peas, potatoes and minced meat and perhaps the best method would be to use some peas left-over from another meal. In any event, feel free to experiment with your fillings, especially for parties.

IMPERIAL/METRIC	AMERICAN
4 oz./100 g. margarine	$\frac{1}{2}$ cup margarine
8 oz./225 g. plain flour	2 cups all-purpose flour
$\frac{1}{2}$ teaspoon salt	$\frac{1}{2}$ teaspoon salt
1 teaspoon black cummin seed	1 teaspoon black cummin seed
$\frac{1}{4}$ pint/1$\frac{1}{2}$ dl. milk	$\frac{2}{3}$ cup milk
vegetable oil	vegetable oil

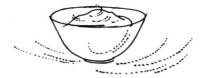

1   *Rub in the dry ingredients with the fat and add the milk to form a dough.*

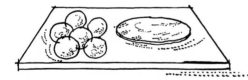

2   *Break off pieces of dough and form into balls 1 inch in diameter. Roll the balls into circles about $\frac{1}{16}$ inch in thickness.*

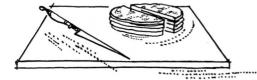

3   *Make a pile of the well-floured circles and with a sharp knife cut through the centre to form semi-circles.*

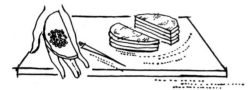

4   *Lay a semi-circle of dough across your palm and place approximately 1 tablespoon of the cooked filling in the centre. Wet one corner of the semicircle with water and fold over to form a triangle shape, press the edges together to seal.*

1   Rub the margarine into the flour together with the salt and cummin seed. It is essential that this rubbing-in process should be carried out thoroughly and that the flour has an homogeneous consistency.

2   Now add the milk and mix until you have a dough which is hard and slightly tacky to the touch. Add more milk or flour to achieve this.

3   Now comes the most difficult part; break off 1-inch balls of dough and roll them on a floury board until you have circles $\frac{1}{16}$ inch in thickness. Repeat this process until you have approximately 25 rounds of pastry.

4   Lay the rounds one on the top of the other making sure each is well floured to prevent sticking. With a sharp knife cut into semi-circles. You are now ready to form the samosas.

5   Have by your side a bowl of flour and a bowl of cold water. Take a semi-circle of pastry and lay it across your right hand, now take approximately 1 tablespoon of the cooked filling and place it in the centre of your palm. Fold over one corner of the semi-circle and stick by wetting slightly with the cold water, transfer to the other hand and complete the folding. You should now have a triangular shaped patty, which you seal by pressing together the moistened sides at the wide end of the triangle. You will probably need five or six attempts to achieve the correct shape, but after that you will find it child's play.

6   It only remains now to fry for about a minute in vegetable oil until golden brown. Samosas may be served either hot or cold and are excellent for deep-frying.

5   *When cooked, the samosas can be served hot or cold.*

Korma is another well-known dish served in Indian restaurants and the most popular korma is lamb. Those who have not tried korma before will appreciate the beautiful sensation of crunching through nuts while you are eating a tasty meat dish, all cooked in a sauce that seems to complement both the flavours – of the nuts and the meat. The secret of korma is the use of saffron; although it may seem very expensive it is the most essential part of this dish. It adds greatly to the delicate flavour.

IMPERIAL/METRIC	AMERICAN
1 lb./450 g. lean lamb	1 lb. lean lamb
½ teaspoon saffron	½ teaspoon saffron
3–4 tablespoons boiling water	¼–⅓ cup boiling water
2 oz./50 g. unsalted cashew nuts	½ cup unsalted cashew nuts
3 green chillis	3 green chilis
1 oz./25 g. fresh ginger	1½ tablespoons chopped fresh ginger
1-inch/2·5-cm. stick cinnamon	1-inch stick cinnamon
½ teaspoon cardamom seed	½ teaspoon cardamom seed
6 cloves	6 cloves
3 cloves garlic	3 cloves garlic
2 teaspoons coriander powder	2 teaspoons coriander powder
½ teaspoon cummin seed	½ teaspoon cummin seed
½ pint/3 dl. water	1¼ cups water
4 oz./100 g. ghee	½ cup ghee
1 large onion	1 large onion
1 teaspoon salt	1 teaspoon salt
½ pint/3 dl. yogurt	1¼ cups yogurt
1 tablespoon chopped fresh coriander	1 tablespoon chopped fresh coriander
2 teaspoons lemon juice	2 teaspoons lemon juice
For garnish	
fresh coriander	fresh coriander

1 Ensure that the lamb is completely free of fat and is cut into 1-inch cubes. Leg or shoulder are the best cuts to get.

2 Place the saffron in a bowl and pour on to it approximately 3 or 4 tablespoons of boiling water. Let it infuse for 10 minutes.

3 Meanwhile, add the cashew nuts, chillis, chopped ginger, cinnamon, cardamoms, cloves, garlic, coriander and cummin seeds to a liquidiser together with ½ pint of water and blend for 2 minutes until you have a smooth purée.

4 Now heat the ghee until very hot (a good test of this is that the water flicked into it splutters instantly). Slice the onions, and fry in the ghee until golden brown. Stir in the salt and the blended spices and the yogurt. Cook gently for about 5 minutes stirring occasionally.

5 Add the lamb pieces turning to ensure that they are well coated. Now add the saffron together with the water in which it has been soaking and reduce the heat to very low. Cook for 20 minutes in a covered pan, stirring occasionally.

6 Add a tablespoon of fresh coriander and cook for another 10 minutes, until the lamb is tender.

7 Serve in a heated dish with lemon juice and garnished with the rest of the coriander.

MUTTON MADRAS

This is one dish for all you fire-eaters and it tastes exactly as it sounds, very hot! I would be very surprised if many people were able to tell what meat is used in this dish. The amounts that I have given here are sufficient to make what I call a hot curry. The more intrepid of you may choose to add even more chillis. Hosts should be very careful if contemplating using this recipe as I know from past experience that there is nothing more calculated to put someone off Indian food for good than a tangle with a very hot curry at the outset of their experience of Indian food. Having said all that, feel free to indulge your personal tastes!

IMPERIAL/METRIC	AMERICAN
1 lb./450 g. mutton	1 lb. mutton
2 oz./50 g. ghee	¼ cup ghee
1 large onion	1 large onion
2 teaspoons garam masala	2 teaspoons garam masala
2 teaspoons chilli powder	2 teaspoons chili powder
3 oz./75 g. tomato purée	generous ¼ cup tomato paste
3 cardamoms	3 cardamoms
1 teaspoon salt	1 teaspoon salt
½ lemon	½ lemon

1 Cut fat from mutton and fry gently in the ghee to seal.

2 Remove the meat and fry the sliced onion along with the garam masala and chilli powder. Stir in well and fry for 4 minutes.

3 Now add the pieces of mutton together with the tomato purée and the crushed cardamoms. Stir well and cover the pan with a close-fitting lid. Simmer gently for about 30 minutes, stirring occasionally. Add water if the curry appears to be dry, but the sauce should be quite thick.

4 Finally, add the salt and the juice from half a lemon. Simmer very slowly for another 15 minutes until the meat is tender. Serve with plain rice.

PORK VINDALOO

It would appear that not many Westerners realise that there is, albeit small, a section of India that does in fact eat pork. It must be stressed, however, that pigs are hardly ever bred as such and a lot of the pork eaten is of the *shikar* type – the wild boar which roams in the sugar-cane plantations. Of course, it is taboo for Muslims to eat pork and for many other religious sects in India; and even for those Indians to whom it is not strictly forbidden, the eating of pork is not encouraged, since the climatic conditions are very favourable to the production of tapeworm. Nonetheless, the few Indians who do eat pork have developed some very exotic and tasty ways of cooking it.

IMPERIAL/METRIC	AMERICAN
2 large onions	2 large onions
8 cloves garlic	8 cloves garlic
6 oz./175 g. ghee	¾ cup ghee
1½ lb./675 g. lean pork	1½ lb. lean pork
½ teaspoon paprika	½ teaspoon paprika pepper
½ teaspoon turmeric	½ teaspoon turmeric
1 teaspoon fenugreek seeds	1 teaspoon fenugreek seeds
1 oz./25 g. fresh ginger	1½ tablespoons chopped fresh ginger
2 green chillis	2 green chilis
1 teaspoon salt	1 teaspoon salt
¼ pint/1½ dl. water	⅔ cup water
2 oz./50 g. tamarind	2 oz. tamarind
1½ teaspoons garam masala	1½ teaspoons garam masala
2 bay leaves	2 bay leaves
6 cardamoms	6 cardamoms
3 cloves	3 cloves

1 Peel and slice the onions and garlic and fry in the ghee. Now take the pork and make sure that it is completely free of fat, cut into 1-inch cubes and fry in a little ghee to seal the juices.

2 Now remove the pot from the heat and add the paprika, turmeric, fenugreek seeds, chopped ginger, green chillis and the salt. Add about ¼ pint of water to this and cook gently for about 20 or 30 minutes in a covered pot until the meat is tender.

4 Meanwhile, soak the tamarind for 30 minutes to form a pulp.

5 Now uncover the pot and bring to the boil and evaporate nearly all the water. Then add the rest of the spices and the tamarind pulp and cook on a very low heat for approximately 30 minutes.

DUM KA MURGH

This is a Madrasee recipe not unlike one of the northern Indian chicken recipes except that the spices used are a lot hotter. You will see that it follows the northern Indian style closely in as much as the bird is rubbed with a spiced preparation beforehand. However, the difference is that the bird is rubbed with the spice and not marinated in a spiced sauce as in northern Indian cooking. This particular method of cooking chicken is perhaps superior in taste even to the famed tandoori chicken. But I will leave you to decide that.

IMPERIAL/METRIC	AMERICAN
1 3-lb./1⅓-kg. oven-ready chicken	1 3-lb. oven-ready chicken
1 lb./450 g. onions	1 lb. onions
4 oz./100 g. ghee	½ cup ghee
¼ pint/1½ dl. yogurt	⅔ cup yogurt
1-inch/2·5-cm. stick cinnamon	1-inch stick cinnamon
½ teaspoon ground black pepper	½ teaspoon ground black pepper
2 cardamoms	2 cardamoms
½ teaspoon chilli powder	½ teaspoon chili powder
2 green chillis	2 green chilis
½ oz./15 g. fresh coriander	⅓ cup fresh coriander
½ teaspoon ground ginger	½ teaspoon ground ginger
2 teaspoons salt	2 teaspoons salt
2 teaspoons desiccated coconut	2 teaspoons shredded coconut

1　Skin and joint the chicken.

2　Slice the onions and fry in the ghee until golden brown.

3　Set aside approximately a quarter of the onion and place the remaining three quarters in a liquidiser together with the yogurt, cinnamon, black pepper, cardamoms, chilli powder, green chillis, coriander leaves, ground ginger, salt and coconut and liquidise for about 3 minutes.

4　Prick the chicken all over with a fork and rub this mixture well into the bird. You should take about 10 minutes doing this. Leave for 4 hours.

5　Heat the oven to 350°F., Gas Mark 4, and arrange the chicken in an oven-proof dish, pour the left-over ghee and the remaining quarter of the onion over the top of the chicken and cook for 1 hour until tender.

CHICKEN VINDALOO

Ask a Westerner for his idea of a hot curry and he will tell you 'Vindaloo'. For it is vindaloo that is served up in most Indian restaurants as the hottest in the house. It must be stressed, however, that vindaloo is a way of cooking and not merely a way of describing something that has a high proportion of green and red chillis in it. Funnily enough, the amount of chillis is not the most important aspect of this style of cooking, and as I have said before, the object of cooking any dish is that you should be able to taste the nuances of flavour. This recipe is somewhat modified for Western taste in as much as I have cut down the number of hot spices used without, I hope, marring the overall effect.

IMPERIAL/METRIC	AMERICAN
1 3-lb./1⅓-kg. oven-ready chicken	1 3-lb. oven-ready chicken
2 large onions	2 large onions
8 oz./225 g. ghee	1 cup ghee
2 green chillis	2 green chilis
1 oz./25 g. fresh ginger	1½ tablespoons chopped fresh ginger
3 cloves garlic	3 cloves garlic
1½ teaspoons turmeric	1½ teaspoons turmeric
1 teaspoon coriander powder	1 teaspoon coriander powder
1 teaspoon garam masala	1 teaspoon garam masala
2 tablespoons vinegar	3 tablespoons vinegar
½ pint/3 dl. water	1¼ cups water
1 teaspoon salt	1 teaspoon salt
2 oz./50 g. desiccated coconut	⅔ cup shredded coconut

1　Skin and joint the chicken (you can do this yourself or get your butcher to do it).

2　Slice the onions and fry in the ghee together with the green chillis. When the onions are golden brown, add the chopped ginger, garlic, turmeric, coriander and garam masala. Fry for a further 3 minutes.

3　Now add the vinegar and the water, together with the chicken pieces. Cover and simmer for about 30 minutes. Test the chicken with a skewer to see if it is cooked; if you get a clear juice coming out of the chicken then it is done.

4　Now remove the lid of the pot and boil rapidly until the gravy thickens and then add the salt and the coconut, simmer for 15 minutes and serve.

STUFFED HALIBUT

This is one of the most famous dishes to come from the Kerala coast. Halibut, pomfret, and other such fish abound in the teeming seas off southern India and every day the natives can be seen fishing with their peculiar see-saw type nets which trap the fish as they swim out from the inlets on the ebb tide. If you are a great fish eater I am sure you will find this a tasty alternative to the usual run-of-the-mill fish dishes.

IMPERIAL/METRIC	AMERICAN
1 2-lb./900-g. halibut	1 2-lb. halibut
1 lemon	1 lemon
1 teaspoon salt	1 teaspoon salt
½ teaspoon paprika	½ teaspoon paprika pepper
1 oz./25 g. blanched almonds	scant ¼ cup blanched almonds
1 oz./25 g. sultanas	3 tablespoons seedless white raisins
2 oz./50 g. ghee	¼ cup ghee
1 large onion	1 large onion
½ teaspoon garam masala	½ teaspoon garam masala
6 oz./175 g. mashed potatoes	¾ cup mashed potato
1 teaspoon chopped fresh ginger	1 teaspoon chopped fresh ginger
½ egg	½ egg
2 green chillis	2 green chilis
1½ teaspoons chopped mint	1½ teaspoons chopped mint
vegetable oil	vegetable oil
For garnish	
tomato slices	tomato slices
lemon slices	lemon slices

Illustrated on page 29.

1 To prepare the fish, wash it all over and remove the eyes and wash out the insides. Do not remove the head. Now take the lemon and rub it all over the fish both inside and outside. Repeat this with some of the salt and the paprika. Leave for about 6 hours.

2 When the 6 hours are almost up, fry the blanched almonds and the sultanas in the ghee and put them to one side. Now fry the onions in the same ghee and then add the garam masala, the rest of the salt and the mashed potatoes. Left-overs are quite adequate for this.

3 Allow to cool and then add the liquidised ginger pulp, the beaten egg, the fried almonds and sultanas and the finely cut green chillis and the mint. Mix well and place this mixture inside the fish; stitch lightly using a few turns of cotton thread.

4 Heat the vegetable oil in a frying pan until it is smoking and then add the fish and fry very quickly until it is crisp.

5 Serve whole, garnished with tomatoes and slices of lemon.

MASALA FRIED FISH

This is another Keralanese dish but it is often a general way to cook any sort of fish. The only requirement of the fish used is that it should be filleted; I often suspect that the heavy spicing used in this recipe would in some catering establishments cover any staleness!

IMPERIAL/METRIC	AMERICAN
1½ lb./675 g. cod fillets	1½ lb. flounder fillets
4 tablespoons vinegar	⅓ cup vinegar
1 teaspoon chilli powder	1 teaspoon chili powder
2 oz./50 g. fresh ginger	3 tablespoons chopped fresh ginger
5 cloves garlic	5 cloves garlic
2 tablespoons lemon juice	3 tablespoons lemon juice
4 oz./100 g. chick-pea flour	1 cup chick-pea flour
vegetable oil	vegetable oil
For garnish	
lemon	lemon
parsley	parsley

1 Cut the fish fillets into 4-inch squares. Soak in the vinegar for 30 minutes.

2 Place the chilli powder, chopped ginger, garlic, and lemon juice in a liquidiser and liquidise for 2 minutes until a smooth paste is obtained. Pour off the vinegar from the fish into the liquidiser and liquidise for a further 30 seconds.

3 Marinate the fish in this mixture for 6 hours.

4 Remove the fish at this point and mix the chick-pea flour in to make a pakora-like batter. Re-dip the fish in the batter and deep-fry in hot oil until golden brown.

5 Serve garnished with lemon and parsley.

PRAWN PATHIA
Curried prawns

This dish is most popular in Indian restaurants in the major cities of the West. Its popularity is probably due to the fact that prawns are considered exotic and expensive in most cases, especially in cities which are a long way from the sea. The original dish of course, used fresh prawns, but most Indian restaurants have to use frozen prawns and this is probably an advantage as it cuts down the risk of food poisoning! However, using frozen prawns which have to be imported from places like Malaya and Bangladesh inflates the price so it is as well to be completely sure of what you are going to do in this dish before you attempt it. When preparing a spiced dish from any sea food which is noted for its delicate flavour, it is obviously essential to ensure that the spicing does not mar this fresh flavour. In my opinion the following recipe for prawn pathia avoids this problem and as long as you do not overcook the prawns you will have a very tasty dish.

Note Because of the fenugreek you will notice that there is none of the fishy smell usually associated with prawn dishes, and the spicing ensures that prawns cooked in this way may be kept in the fridge for three or four days and reheated without any fear of the prawns going bad.

IMPERIAL/METRIC	AMERICAN
2 large onions	2 large onions
8 oz./225 g. ghee	1 cup ghee
2 oz./50 g. desiccated coconut	⅔ cup shredded coconut
1 teaspoon chilli powder	1 teaspoon chili powder
2 teaspoons paprika	2 teaspoons paprika pepper
1-inch/2·5-cm. stick cinnamon	1-inch stick cinnamon
2 bay leaves	2 bay leaves
1 teaspoon garam masala	1 teaspoon garam masala
2 teaspoons fenugreek	2 teaspoons fenugreek
1 oz./25 g. fresh ginger	2 teaspoons finely sliced ginger
4 oz./100 g. tomato purée	scant ½ cup tomato paste
½ pint/3 dl. yogurt	1¼ cups yogurt
1 lb./450 g. prawns (shelled weight)	1 cup peeled shrimp

Illustrated on page 53.

1 Fry the onions in the ghee until golden brown.

2 Now add the desiccated coconut and cook until it also is golden brown. When cooking with coconut it is essential to remember two things. Firstly, the coconut must not be of too fine a consistency (stipulate medium or coarse grade when purchasing) and secondly that when you are cooking it that none of it sticks to the bottom of the pan.

3 Stir in the chilli powder, paprika, cinnamon, bay leaves, garam masala, fenugreek, and ginger (if using fresh ginger slice it finely first), and then add the tomato purée and yogurt. Stir in well and if necessary add a little hot water to make the sauce the consistency of thickened yogurt.

4 When the mixture boils add the prawns immediately, turning down the heat, and simmer very slowly in a covered pot until the prawns are cooked. This could take anything from 15 to 30 minutes, depending on how thawed out the prawns were. If you find the sauce is too liquid remove the saucepan lid to allow some of the water to evaporate.

JHINGHE KA TIKKA
Minced prawn curry balls

This recipe uses minced prawns and although this may seem a terrible waste of prawns to those who pay such a high price for them, I am sure you will find this a very interesting way of serving seafood. Again, one may use either fresh or frozen prawns, the latter probably being both more economic and safer to use. This is one of those Indian dishes which one can serve with ordinary Western accompaniments like mashed potatoes and peas.

IMPERIAL/METRIC	AMERICAN
12 oz./350 g. prawns (shelled weight)	1½ cups peeled shrimp
2 cloves garlic	2 cloves garlic
1 heaped tablespoon chopped ginger	1½ tablespoons chopped ginger
1 green chilli	1 green chili
1 large onion	1 large onion
½ teaspoon turmeric	½ teaspoon turmeric
½ teaspoon ground black pepper	½ teaspoon ground black pepper
½ teaspoon salt	½ teaspoon salt
1 egg	1 egg
breadcrumbs to coat	bread crumbs to coat
4 oz./100 g. butter	½ cup butter
For garnish	
unshelled prawns, mint or parsley	unpeeled shrimp, mint or parsley

1 Run the prawns through a mincer together with the garlic, ginger, chilli, onion, turmeric, black pepper and salt. It is essential to use the finest blade on the mincer or alternatively use a liquidiser but be careful not to reduce the mixture to a liquid pulp.

2 Now mix in the egg and form into round croquettes approximately 2 inches in diameter. Coat with the breadcrumbs, fry in the butter until golden brown on all sides, turning once. This should take approximately 6 or 7 minutes.

3 The essential thing with all fried foods is that they should be garnished nicely; with this dish especially it is necessary to make it attractive. Perhaps one could put aside a few whole, unpeeled prawns or failing that, a few sprigs of mint or parsley make all the difference.

HOPPERS

Hoppers are very similar to dosas and in my opinion are one of the most interesting dishes to come out of south India. They are a typical Madras dish, the difference from dosa being that they use only rice flour and no dal, and coconut milk instead of water to prepare the batter. Originally hoppers were cooked in earthenware pots with rounded bottoms known as *hopper-chattis*, which were placed in the ashes of a slow charcoal fire. The hopper batter would be poured in and the chatti quickly spun to make the batter swirl around into the hotter parts of the vessel. This would give a lacy crisp border to the pancake. The centre of the hopper is somewhat thicker than the dosa. This method of cooking is a very skilful one, but it is something that can be emulated in the Western kitchen by using a small omelette pan and swirling the batter so that it runs up the sides. Alternatively, one can use a metal *kurhai* which has two handles to facilitate the swirling process. These kurhais are completely curved and can be bought in either Chinese or Indian shops.

IMPERIAL/METRIC	AMERICAN
8 oz./225 g. best Basmati rice	generous cup best Basmati rice
1 teaspoon salt	1 teaspoon salt
¼ pint/1½ dl. coconut milk	⅔ cup coconut milk
pinch bicarbonate soda	pinch baking soda
little butter	little butter

1 Grind the rice using a coffee mill or a mortar and pestle, and mix together with the salt and the coconut milk and a pinch of bicarbonate of soda. Leave overnight. In the morning whip the batter so that there is plenty of air in it. This has the effect of making the hoppers light.

2 Next grease the cooking vessel with a little butter. Put the cooking vessel on a medium heat and pour in a little of the batter. As soon as the batter is poured in spin the vessel so that the batter runs up the side.

3 Immediately the batter becomes hard in the middle remove with a fish slice. Store in a warm cloth. Hoppers are usually eaten at breakfast or teatime.

KHEER
Rice pudding

Kheer is essentially a rice pudding but it is far superior to the one we are served in the West. As I have said in the Introduction, when talking about rice cooking, patna rice is only suitable for making rice pudding and so perhaps one could use up patna rice for this dish. It is a great favourite for parties as it is best served cold from the fridge.

Note In India kheer and other sweet dishes are usually served decorated with very thin leaves of pure silver. If you can get hold of some from your local Indian suppliers then your kheer will be that much more attractive – not to say more expensive. This silver foil is not only edible but some people hold that it is an aid to digestion.

IMPERIAL/METRIC	AMERICAN
3 oz./75 g. rice	$\frac{1}{2}$ cup rice
$\frac{1}{4}$ pint/1$\frac{1}{2}$ dl. water	$\frac{2}{3}$ cup water
3 pints/1$\frac{1}{2}$ litres milk	3$\frac{3}{4}$ pints milk
6 oz./175 g. sugar	$\frac{3}{4}$ cup sugar
2 cardamoms	2 cardamoms
3–4 drops kewra water	3–4 drops kewra water
$\frac{1}{2}$ oz./15 g. blanched almonds	1 tablespoon blanched almonds
2 oz./50 g. raisins	$\frac{1}{3}$ cup raisins
For garnish	
finely beaten silver foil	finely beaten silver foil

Illustrated on page 60.

1 Soak the rice in approximately $\frac{1}{4}$ pint of water for 30 minutes. Then bring to the boil and boil until the water dries up.

2 Now add the milk to the saucepan and stir the rice, keeping on a very low heat for 1$\frac{1}{2}$ hours. During the time keep scraping the bottom and sides of the pan until you have a creamy consistency and then add the sugar.

3 When you have a perfect consistency remove from the heat and add the crushed cardamoms, kewra water, almonds and raisins.

4 Pour into small dishes and allow to set in the fridge.

PAYASAM

Payasam is another of the Indian milk-based sweets. This dish uses sago to give a creamy consistency along with vermicelli and desiccated coconut. As it is quite complicated to make, it is a dish usually reserved for feast days.

IMPERIAL/METRIC	AMERICAN
2 oz./50 g. sago	$\frac{1}{3}$ cup sago
$\frac{1}{2}$ pint/3 dl. water	1$\frac{1}{4}$ cups water
5 cardamoms	5 cardamoms
1 teaspoon melted ghee	1 teaspoon melted ghee
2 pints/1$\frac{1}{4}$ litres milk	2$\frac{1}{2}$ pints milk
2 oz./50 g. sugar	scant $\frac{1}{4}$ cup sugar
2 oz./50 g. vermicelli	2 oz. vermicelli
2 oz./50 g. desiccated coconut	$\frac{2}{3}$ cup shredded coconut
2 oz./50 g. sultanas	$\frac{1}{3}$ cup seedless white raisins
For garnish	
pistachios	pistachios

1 Soak the sago for 1 hour in $\frac{1}{2}$ pint of water.

2 Fry the cardamoms in the ghee in a large saucepan and add the milk and sugar.

3 Bring to the boil, simmer for 10 minutes, stirring constantly to ensure that the sugar is dissolved. Now drain the sago and add, stirring for a further 5 minutes.

4 Now add the vermicelli and stir for 2 minutes.

5 Finally add the coconut and sultanas and boil, simmer for 5 minutes.

6 Serve garnished with pistachios.

CONCLUSION ON SOUTHERN INDIA

Unlike in north India, the vegetable dishes of the south are usually taken as the main course. Thus baigan masalewala, bhagare baigan and goodhi bhajis all form light vegetarian meals, together with lashings of plain boiled Basmati rice. When serving fish dishes it is always advisable to have plenty of lemon on hand as some of these dishes can be quite oily. Lamb korma and vindaloo are best served with rice, and aviyal as an ancillary dish. End with kheer or payasam.

EAST INDIA

The majority of Indian restaurants in the Western world are run by east Indians, mainly Bengalis. It is not surprising therefore that the dishes served in those restaurants are mainly of an east Indian origin.

This chapter includes dishes from Bengal and Bihar. Bengal is very similar to Kerala in as much as its waters abound with many varieties of fish. Unfortunately, a lot of the fish to be found in the rivers and estuaries of Bengal are not to be had in the western waters so this chapter contains relatively few fish dishes. Bengalis do not eat fish only and you will find many non-fish recipes here which are equally as tasty.

East Indian cooks are renowned for their mastery of cooking with Indian cream cheese and it is certainly in these cheese dishes, both savoury and sweet, that the east Indians excel. It is appropriate, therefore, that the first recipe in this chapter is for Indian cream cheese, known as panir or chenna.

PANIR

IMPERIAL/METRIC	AMERICAN
2 pints/generous litre milk	2½ pints milk
1 tablespoon lemon juice	1 tablespoon lemon juice
or 4 tablespoons yogurt	or ⅓ cup yogurt

1 Place the milk in a large saucepan and bring to the boil, stirring continuously so that no skin forms on top of the milk. When the milk boils, remove from the heat and while allowing it to cool, gradually add the lemon juice or yogurt, stirring all the time until the milk has curdled completely.

2 Now cover and leave for 15 minutes.

3 Next, strain through a muslin cloth, squeezing well to extract all the watery whey. The loose curds that you are now left with in the cloth are known as chenna.

4 This is the form usually used for making sweets. However, some savoury recipes call for cubes of Indian cream cheese, and so to obtain these it is necessary to compress the chenna into a slab to form panir. This is done by wrapping the curds in a cloth and compressing between a few old books so there is a weight of approximately 7 lb. on the cheese. You will find that the cheese will have compressed into a slab after about 2½ hours. This slab can then be cut into cubes and stored in a refrigerator.

Of all the savoury dishes with cream cheese, the most popular is matar panir. Its popularity is mainly due to the fact that it is one of the few Indian cream cheese dishes served in Indian restaurants. It is quite easy to make at home once you have prepared the cream cheese.

IMPERIAL/METRIC	AMERICAN
whey remaining from making panir	whey remaining from making panir
8 oz./225 g. panir	1 cup panir
4 oz./100 g. ghee	½ cup ghee
½ teaspoon salt	½ teaspoon salt
2 large onions	2 large onions
¼ pint/1½ dl. water	⅔ cup water
8 oz./225 g. frozen peas	1½ cups frozen peas
½ teaspoon paprika	½ teaspoon paprika pepper
½ teaspoon ground ginger	½ teaspoon ground ginger
½ teaspoon garam masala	½ teaspoon garam masala

Illustrated opposite.

1. For this recipe it is essential to save the watery whey formed in making the panir (see page 47). Cut the panir into ½-inch cubes and fry in the ghee until they are a light brown colour. Remove from the ghee and leave to soak for 15 minutes in the whey and the salt.

2. Now take the onions and slice them finely; fry in the same ghee until golden brown. Remove the onions and keep to one side.

3. Add the water to the pot and then add the peas. Cover and cook for about 3–4 minutes until the peas are almost cooked and then drain.

4. Now add the onions, panir cubes, paprika and ginger and stir very gently for 2 to 3 minutes.

5. Finally add the garam masala, stirring for 2 minutes and serve immediately.

EKOORI

Ekoori is a dish peculiar to the Parsees, who live on the west coast and in east India. Basically this dish is an Indian version of scrambled eggs. However, I am sure when you prepare it you will find that it is quite a change from the normal jaundiced dish that is prepared in the West.

IMPERIAL/METRIC	AMERICAN
1 small onion	1 small onion
4 oz./100 g. ghee	½ cup ghee
1 oz./25 g. fresh ginger	1½ tablespoons finely sliced fresh ginger
1 green chilli	1 green chili
½ teaspoon salt	½ teaspoon salt
½ teaspoon ground black pepper	½ teaspoon ground black pepper
½ teaspoon turmeric	½ teaspoon turmeric
8 eggs	8 eggs
	For garnish
fresh coriander	fresh coriander
tomatoes	tomatoes

1. Slice the onion finely and fry in the ghee until golden brown using a heavy frying pan.

2. Meanwhile, scrape the ginger and slice it into fine strips. Similarly slice the green chilli. Add both of these to the onion and cook for 3 minutes.

3. Now add the salt, black pepper and turmeric and stir in for a further 2 minutes.

4. Beat the eggs, reduce the heat and add to the frying pan, stirring very briskly. Keep scraping the sides and bottom of the pan until you have your scrambled eggs.

5. Serve garnished with fresh coriander and tomatoes.

Calcutta beef curry (page 50), and matir panir

Calcutta lies in the state of West Bengal, far in the east of India. With its teeming population it used to be described as the cesspool of India in view of the inadequate sanitary conditions. But despite this defamatory title it produces some very good cooking. The following recipe is a typical dish of Calcutta, being basically a curry prepared with a thin gravy which has a high proportion of ghee in it. It is a very useful way of using up any of the poorer quality cuts of meat and for the following recipe shin of beef can be used with confidence.

IMPERIAL/METRIC	AMERICAN
1 lb./450 g. beef	1 lb. beef
1 pint/6 dl. water	2½ cups water
2 teaspoons coriander powder	2 teaspoons coriander powder
½ teaspoon turmeric	½ teaspoon turmeric
½ teaspoon cummin seed powder	½ teaspoon cummin seed powder
1 teaspoon chilli powder	1 teaspoon chili powder
½ teaspoon ground black pepper	½ teaspoon ground black pepper
2 teaspoons salt	2 teaspoons salt
1 teaspoon ground ginger	1 teaspoon ground ginger
little milk to mix	little milk to mix
1 large onion	1 large onion
1 clove garlic	1 clove garlic
1 oz./25 g. ghee	2 tablespoons ghee
For garnish	
fresh coriander or parsley	fresh coriander or parsley

1 Clean all the beef of any fat, cut into 1½-inch chunks and simmer in the lightly salted water until tender.

2 Mix together the coriander powder, turmeric, cummin seed powder, chilli powder, black pepper, salt and ginger to make a paste, using a little milk.

3 Peel the onion and slice thinly along with the garlic. Fry in the ghee until golden brown. Add the paste and fry for a further 3 minutes.

4 Now add the meat together with half the water in which it has been boiling. Bring to the boil and simmer for 15 minutes, adding some of the remaining water if the gravy appears too thick.

5 Serve garnished with a little chopped green coriander or parsley.

Illustrated on page 49.

TALI KALEJA

Kaleja is the Indian name for liver, and tali means fried. So 'tali kaleja' literally translated means fried liver. However, I am sure you will find this method of cooking liver far superior to most Western recipes, as it brings out the flavour of the liver without allowing it to become too dry. Of course, in India, lambs' livers are generally used, but there is nothing to stop you using chicken or even pigs' livers.

IMPERIAL/METRIC	AMERICAN
1 small onion	1 small onion
some mustard oil for cooking	some mustard oil for cooking
½ teaspoon turmeric	½ teaspoon turmeric
½ teaspoon chilli powder	½ teaspoon chili powder
½ teaspoon ground black pepper	½ teaspoon ground black pepper
½ teaspoon ground ginger	½ teaspoon ground ginger
½ teaspoon salt	½ teaspoon salt
½ lb./225 g. liver	½ lb. liver
1 clove garlic	1 clove garlic
For garnish	
tomatoes	tomatoes

1 Slice the onion and fry gently in the mustard oil using a heavy frying pan.

2 Mix the turmeric, chilli powder, black pepper and ground ginger with the salt and make this into a paste with a little water.

3 Cut the liver into ¼-inch thick slices, wash well and then having dried the slices, rub the spice paste into each slice.

4 Add together with the garlic to the pan, cover and cook for 10 minutes until the liver is tender.

5 Serve garnished with tomatoes.

MUCHLI MOLEE

Molee is the name given to dishes cooked with a basis of thick coconut milk. Molee dishes are usually found in the south and east of India and on the Ceylonese coast where it is most normal to prepare food in this way. In general, cooked fish is used to prepare a molee dish and this could perhaps be a good opportunity for you to use up any left-over fish pie. The only difficult ingredient needed is the coconut milk which can be bought from an Indian suppliers or can be made by grating out the inside of a fresh coconut and pouring approximately ½ pint of boiling water onto it. When this has been set aside for 30 minutes and strained then you will have a fairly thick coconut milk. In the following recipe it would be quite permissible to use frozen cod steaks.

IMPERIAL/METRIC	AMERICAN
1 large onion	1 large onion
1 clove garlic	1 clove garlic
2 oz./50 g. ghee	¼ cup ghee
3 green chillis	3 green chilis
1 teaspoon turmeric	1 teaspoon turmeric
1 pint/6 dl. coconut milk	2½ cups coconut milk
2 tablespoons vinegar	3 tablespoons vinegar
1 lb./450 g. cooked fish	1 lb. cooked fish
For garnish	
coriander leaves	coriander leaves
ground ginger	ground ginger

1 Take a deep frying pan and fry the finely sliced onion and garlic in the ghee.

2 Next, remove the stalks of the chillis and cut lengthwise in halves. Fry these also, being careful not to allow any of the ingredients to brown.

3 Now add the turmeric and cook for 4 minutes on a very low heat.

4 Finally, add the coconut milk and vinegar and simmer gently for 10 minutes.

5 Now place the fish in the sauce and allow it to warm thoroughly. If you are using whole fish it is advisable not to stir as they will quite easily break up.

6 Garnish with coriander leaves and sprinkle with ground ginger.

KELA KOFTA

This recipe makes use of green bananas which may not be too easy to get hold of. It is well worth it if you can as this is an exotic and different dish which has no counterpart in Western cuisine.

IMPERIAL/METRIC	AMERICAN
1½ lb./675 g. green bananas	1½ lb. green bananas
3 oz./75 g. ghee	⅓ cup ghee
1 small onion	1 small onion
2 cloves garlic	2 cloves garlic
½ teaspoon ground ginger	½ teaspoon ground ginger
1 teaspoon salt	1 teaspoon salt
1 teaspoon paprika	1 teaspoon paprika pepper
3 cardamoms	3 cardamoms
1 egg	1 egg
4 tablespoons double cream	⅓ cup heavy cream
3 oz./75 g. tomato purée	generous ¼ cup tomato paste
pinch salt	pinch salt
1 tablespoon ghee	1½ tablespoons ghee

1 Boil the bananas for about 10 minutes in their skins until they become tender. Remove from the heat and allow to cool, then remove the skins and mash the bananas thoroughly.

2 Heat the ghee and fry the onion, garlic and ginger.

3 Now add the banana pulp along with the salt, paprika, and cardamoms, stirring well. Allow to cool.

4 Mix in the egg until you have a soft, pliable dough; shape the mixture into balls approximately an inch in diameter and place on one side.

5 Now put the cream and tomato purée in a saucepan together with a pinch of salt and a little ghee and simmer, stirring constantly. Add the koftas to this mixture and heat gently until ready to serve.

Cachumber (page 65), and mushroom palao (page 55)

Plain boiled rice (page 6), and curried prawns (page 44)

This recipe makes use of whole Bengal beans, otherwise known as Egyptian lentils. It is just one of the many dals that are served all over India, but in my opinion it is the most tasty and also the easiest to prepare as it uses just a pinch each of the usual Indian ingredients.

IMPERIAL/METRIC	AMERICAN
8 oz./225 g. Egyptian lentils	$\frac{1}{2}$ lb. Egyptian lentils
1 pint/6 dl. water	2$\frac{1}{2}$ cups water
1 small onion	1 small onion
1 clove garlic	1 clove garlic
2 oz./50 g. ghee	4 tablespoons ghee
1 teaspoon coriander powder	1 teaspoon coriander powder
1 teaspoon turmeric	1 teaspoon turmeric
$\frac{1}{2}$ teaspoon cummin seed powder	$\frac{1}{2}$ teaspoon cummin seed powder
$\frac{1}{2}$ teaspoon chilli powder	$\frac{1}{2}$ teaspoon chili powder
1 teaspoon fenugreek powder	1 teaspoon fenugreek powder
little vinegar to mix	little vinegar to mix

1 Wash the lentils well, using four or five changes of water. Boil for approximately 10 minutes in the lightly salted water. The lentils should just begin to be tender.

2 Now fry the finely sliced onion and garlic in the ghee in the bottom of a heavy saucepan.

3 While the onions and the garlic are frying, mix the remaining powdered ingredients into a stiff paste with a little vinegar, then add the paste and fry for a further 3 or 4 minutes.

4 Now drain the lentils and add to the pan; simmer for 10 minutes.

5 Serve immediately.

Kitcheree is a dish prepared with rice and lentils. It must be stressed that any spicing is to enhance the flavour of these two ingredients. The following recipe is a general one, making use of the yellow moong dal variety of lentils.

IMPERIAL/METRIC	AMERICAN
8 oz./225 g. best Basmati rice	generous cup best Basmati rice
8 oz./225 g. yellow moong dal	1 cup yellow moong dal
3 oz./75 g. ghee	$\frac{1}{3}$ cup ghee
1 clove garlic	1 clove garlic
5 cloves	5 cloves
5 cardamoms	5 cardamoms
2-inch/5-cm. stick cinnamon	2-inch stick cinnamon
1 small onion	1 small onion
1 teaspoon turmeric	1 teaspoon turmeric
$\frac{1}{2}$ teaspoon salt	$\frac{1}{2}$ teaspoon salt
For garnish	
hard-boiled egg	hard-cooked egg

1 Mix the rice and dal together and wash thoroughly in cold water using at least five changes of water. Pick out all the stones and other bits and pieces. Allow to soak in some cold water for 1 hour.

2 Take a large saucepan with a close-fitting lid and add the ghee together with the finely sliced garlic, cloves, cardamoms, and cinnamon. Fry gently for about a minute.

3 Slice the onion and fry for a further minute in the ghee but do not allow the onions to brown.

4 Next, drain the rice and lentils and add to the saucepan, together with the turmeric and salt. Toss all this gently using a wooden spoon over a very low heat for about 4 or 5 minutes.

5 Meanwhile, have some water boiling, sufficient to cover the rice and when the 4 to 5 minutes are up, add this boiling water and cover the rice plus an inch.

6 Cover with a lid and simmer for approximately 30–45 minutes so that all the moisture is absorbed and the rice is cooked.

7 Serve garnished with slices of hard-boiled egg.

BAIGAN BOORTHA

Boortha is a typically Muslim dish which is often served with palao rice and kitcheree. The taste is more correctly described as savoury rather than the hot spicy taste associated with vegetable curries. As such, it provides an interesting alternative to the usual vegetable dishes served alongside Indian meals. As with most other styles of cooking all manner of vegetables can be used and the following recipe uses aubergines as I think that this is one of the best tasting vegetables when cooked in this way. It would be interesting to compare the flavour of baigan boortha to baigan masalewala in the previous chapter and baigan tamatar in the chapter on northern India. I am sure you will agree that one vegetable can take many different flavours without losing its fresh taste.

IMPERIAL/METRIC	AMERICAN
1 lb./450 g. aubergines	1 lb. eggplants
1 large onion	1 large onion
2 green chillis	2 green chilis
1 tablespoon desiccated coconut	1 tablespoon shredded coconut
1 teaspoon sesame seed oil	1 teaspoon sesame seed oil
1 teaspoon salt	1 teaspoon salt
2 teaspoons lemon juice	2 teaspoons lemon juice
For garnish	
chopped parsley	chopped parsley

Illustrated on page 64.

1 It is necessary to pre-cook the aubergines by either boiling in salted water or baking in a medium oven.

2 When they have become fully tender remove the skins and mash the aubergines into a pulp and add the finely minced onion together with the green chillis.

3 Transfer the pulp into a saucepan and gently cook for about 3 minutes.

4 Add the desiccated coconut together with the sesame seed oil, salt and lemon juice. Cook for 10 minutes and serve sprinkled with chopped parsley.

MUSHROOM PALAO

Mushrooms only grow properly in the temperature climes of the far north of India, and mushroom palao is one of those dishes that has really been born out of demand by Western palates for mushrooms. The recipe is very similar to that for ordinary palao rice, but it must be remembered that in order to preserve the delicate flavour, the mushrooms must not be over-cooked.

IMPERIAL/METRIC	AMERICAN
2 oz./50 g. ghee	$\frac{1}{4}$ cup ghee
2 medium onions	2 medium onions
6 cardamoms	6 cardamoms
6 cloves	6 cloves
1 teaspoon cummin seed	1 teaspoon cummin seed
1 teaspoon black peppercorns	1 teaspoon black peppercorns
1 teaspoon salt	1 teaspoon salt
8 oz./225 g. mushrooms	$\frac{1}{2}$ lb. mushrooms
1 lb./450 g. best Basmati rice	$2\frac{1}{4}$ cups best Basmati rice
2 pints/generous litre water	$2\frac{1}{2}$ pints water

Illustrated on page 52.

1 Put the ghee into a large saucepan over a medium heat. Slice and fry the onions adding the cardamoms, cloves, cummin seeds, black peppercorns and salt after about a minute. Continue to fry, stirring well for about 2 minutes.

2 Now add the chopped mushrooms. The pan should be shaken not stirred as stirring would tend to break the mushrooms. Fry for about 2 minutes. Now remove the mushrooms using a perforated spoon, trying to avoid removing the spices.

3 Add the washed rice to the saucepan immediately followed by the water. Bring to the boil, cover and cook gently for 15 minutes. By this time a lot of the water should have been absorbed.

4 Now add the mushrooms stirring in gently and continue to cook until the rice is soft.

5 Drain off any excess water. Keep in a hot oven until you are ready to serve the meal. A damp cloth over the top of the rice will prevent the rice drying out on the surface.

Aubergines cooked with tomatoes (page 11), palao rice (page 58), and curried meatballs (page 10)

KESARI CHAVAL
Saffron rice

Most people probably know this dish by its English name which is saffron rice. This is the beautiful yellow rice that is nearly always served in Indian restaurants, often under the name of palao. However, to lump it with the other forms of rice would be doing it a grave injustice; this rice stands in a class of its own. It certainly makes an eye-catching centre piece at a dinner party.

IMPERIAL/METRIC	AMERICAN
8 oz./225 g. best Basmati rice	generous cup best Basmati rice
½ teaspoon saffron	½ teaspoon saffron
2 tablespoons boiling water	3 tablespoons boiling water
4 oz./100 g. ghee	½ cup ghee
1-inch/2·5-cm. stick cinnamon	1-inch stick cinnamon
3 cloves	3 cloves
2 large onions	2 large onions
1 pint/6 dl. water	2½ cups water
1 teaspoon salt	1 teaspoon salt
2 cardamom seeds	2 cardamom seeds
For garnish	
silver leaf	silver leaf

1 Wash the rice well and then drain thoroughly.

2 Now place the saffron in a small cup and pour over it about 2 tablespoons of boiling water. Soak for about 10 minutes.

3 While the saffron is soaking put the ghee in a heavy pot and then add the cinnamon, cloves and finely sliced onions. Fry for about 10 minutes, turning constantly to ensure that none of the ingredients stick to the pan.

4 Now turn the heat to very low and add the rice stirring for about 5 minutes until each grain of rice has the same delicate, golden yellow colour.

5 Meanwhile, have boiling approximately a pint of water, together with the salt and cardamom seeds. Add this to the rice and bring rapidly to the boil. Reduce the heat and add the saffron, together with the water in which it has been soaking and stir in gently. Cover and simmer for 25 minutes until the rice has absorbed all the liquid.

6 Serve garnished with silver leaf.

PALAO RICE

Those of you who eat regularly in Indian restaurants may be somewhat confused as to what is and what is not palao rice. This is because of the custom in some of the less scrupulous restaurants to serve up plain boiled rice that has been coloured bright yellow under the title of palao rice. In fact, true palao rice needs, not surprisingly, to be cooked in a particular way and has no added colouring. The idea is to bring out the flavour of the rice itself by adding tinges of other flavourings such as cloves, cumin seeds and cardamoms.

IMPERIAL/METRIC	AMERICAN
1 lb./450 g. best Basmati rice	2¼ cups best Basmati rice
2 oz./50 g. ghee	¼ cup ghee
2 medium onions	2 medium onions
6 cloves	6 cloves
6 cardamoms	6 cardamoms
1 teaspoon black peppercorns	1 teaspoon black peppercorns
1 teaspoon cummin seeds	1 teaspoon cummin seeds
½ teaspoon salt	½ teaspoon salt
2 pints/generous litre water	2½ pints water

1 Wash the rice well being sure to remove stones and anything else that may have found its way into the rice.

2 Place the ghee in a large saucepan over a medium heat. Slice the onions and fry in the ghee for about a minute.

3 Add the cloves, cardamoms, peppercorns and cummin seeds together with the salt. Fry for a further 2 minutes.

4 Reduce the heat and add the rice immediately followed by the water. Bring to the boil and cook gently until the rice is soft, about 20 to 30 minutes.

5 Drain off any excess water and place in a hot oven covered with a damp tea towel until ready to serve.

Illustrated on page 56.

Rasgullah is the best and probably the most famous sweet to come out of east India, being available in most Indian restaurants in the West. The recipe calls for the use of the Indian cream cheese outlined at the beginning of the chapter. The success of this dish depends on the special syrup which is made.

Note Rasgullahs can be kept in a refrigerator for quite a long time but should be stored in a closed container as the syrup will take up other smells in the fridge.

IMPERIAL/METRIC	AMERICAN
2 pints/generous litre milk	2½ pints milk
2 tablespoons lemon juice	3 tablespoons lemon juice
2 lb./900 g. sugar	4 cups sugar
2 pints/generous litre water	2½ pints water
½ lemon	½ lemon
6 cloves	6 cloves
6 cardamoms	6 cardamoms
2 teaspoons rose water	2 teaspoons rose water

1 Make the 2 pints of milk into chenna as indicated at the beginning of the chapter, using the lemon juice. Strain the curds through a coarse cloth and squeeze until very dry.

2 Knead the curds well into little balls about the size of a marble and place on a sheet of greaseproof paper. Put aside.

3 Now prepare the syrup. Add the sugar to 2 pints of boiling water, together with the lemon cut into small pieces, the cloves, cardamoms and rose water. Bring to the boil and ensure that the sugar is completely dissolved; boil until you have obtained a heavy syrup.

4 Allow this to cool and drop the small cheese balls into the syrup. Chill and serve.

MEETA PALAO

Literally translated, meeta palao means sweet rice, and as you would expect this dish takes the form of ordinary rice with added flavour. Meeta palao is one of the most popular dishes in east India where rice is freely available and it is an inexpensive sweet to prepare and it can be served either hot or cold. In my opinion it is best served steaming hot straight from the oven. It is very easy to make as all the ingredients are readily obtainable.

IMPERIAL/METRIC	AMERICAN
1 lb./450 g. best Basmati rice	2¼ cups best Basmati rice
8 oz./225 g. ghee	1 cup ghee
6 cloves	6 cloves
6 cardamoms	6 cardamoms
2-inch/5-cm. stick cinnamon	2-inch stick cinnamon
4 oz./100 g. sultanas	⅔ cup seedless white raisins
2 oz./50 g. blanched almonds	½ cup blanched almonds
2 oz./50 g. pistachios	½ cup pistachios
½ teaspoon saffron	½ teaspoon saffron
¼ pint/1½ dl. water	⅔ cup water
4 oz./100 g. castor sugar	½ cup fine granulated sugar
For garnish	
blanched almonds	blanched almonds
pistachios	pistachios

1 Wash the rice well and soak in cold water for 2 hours.

2 Now take the ghee and melt in a heavy pan and fry the cloves, cardamoms, and cinnamon for 2 or 3 minutes. Then add the sultanas, almonds and pistachios and fry for a further 2 or 3 minutes.

3 While this is being done, soak the saffron in ¼ pint of water. Pour this water together with the saffron into the pan.

4 Next drain the rice and add to the frying pan, turning gently for another 10 minutes.

5 Add enough hot water to cover the rice, place a tight-fitting lid on the pan and continue to cook slowly until all the water has been absorbed and the rice has been cooked.

6 Finally stir in the sugar and serve garnished with blanched almonds and pistachios.

Sewaian (page 62), and rice pudding (page 46)

Sharbet sandal (page 62), mango ice cream (page 31), and pistachio ice cream (page 72)

Sewaian is a sweet vermicelli dish peculiar to Muslims all over India. On the various religious festivals it is customary for the lady of each Muslim household to prepare this dish and send portions of it to friends and relations, garnished with finely-beaten gold or silver. Vermicelli is usually available in most Italian or French grocers as well as Indian stockists.

IMPERIAL/METRIC	AMERICAN
2 oz./50 g. ghee	4 tablespoons ghee
8 cardamoms	8 cardamoms
8 cloves	8 cloves
8 oz./225 g. vermicelli	½ lb. vermicelli
1 pint/6 dl. milk	2½ cups milk
8 oz./225 g. sugar	1 cup sugar
2 oz./50 g. almonds, chopped	¼ cup chopped almonds
2 oz./50 g. pistachios, chopped	¼ cup chopped pistachios
2 teaspoons rose water	2 teaspoons rose water

1 Melt the ghee in a heavy saucepan. Crush the cardamoms and cloves with a rolling pin and fry in the ghee for 2 minutes.

2 Now add the vermicelli, being careful not to break it. Fry until it is golden brown in colour.

3 Now add the milk and stir gently but thoroughly. Cover the pan and cook on a medium heat for approximately 10 minutes, stirring occasionally. It is very important not to be too harsh and break the vermicelli when stirring.

4 When the milk is almost dried up add the sugar with the almonds, pistachios and rose water. Stir in well and allow to cool. Sewaian can be served either hot or cold, but in my opinion it is best when it is ice cold.

Illustrated on page 60.

SHARBET SANDAL

Beverages seem to the average Westerner to be in rather short supply in the Indian cuisine, probably because most Indian restaurants do not go out of their way to provide authentic Indian beverages; this is for two reasons. One is that most restaurants, in order to survive, have to serve the usual quota of wine with the meal to make a profit, and also a lot of the drinks taken in India are made of fresh fruits which are either unavailable or too expensive in the West. There are, however, some drinks which can be made quite cheaply; sharbet sandal is one of these.

Basically it makes use of sandalwood powder or essence (essence is better) and which is supposed to be very effective as a thirst-quencher during hot weather. Sharbet sandal makes a good accompaniment to Indian food. Just make the sharbet up to the maker's instructions and serve with a slice of lemon.

Illustrated on page 61.

CONCLUSION ON EASTERN INDIA

As with southern India vegetables are the order for main dishes in east India, along with plenty of rice. Kesari chaval (saffron rice), is very popular when giving a dinner party. If you decorate a large dish of this with rings of green pepper, tomatoes and sliced hard-boiled egg it can form an attractive centrepiece at your dinner table. Even ekoori when garnished with parsley and sprinkled with garam masala can be quite an acceptable cheap dinner party dish. For a sweet it is probably best to serve sewaian or rasgullah, but remember if you want to serve the meeta palao, not to serve too much rice with the main course, otherwise you will have to widen the doors to allow your guests to leave!

WEST INDIA

The cuisine of west India centres mainly on the flourishing seaport of Bombay. This city has given its name to a number of well-known Indian dishes including Bombay duck and Bombay halwa. Bombay itself is a very cosmopolitan city, thus the cuisine which has developed around this area includes dishes from many parts of India. The other major style of cooking in western India is from Goa, situated in two parts, a little to the north and south of Bombay and has been inhabited from early times by a large number of Catholics as well as Muslims and Hindus. Goanese cooking is very different from the Bombay style but both retain an essential western Indian flavour.

KHAT MITHI GOBI

Literally translated, this dish is 'sweet and sour cabbage'. In India, whenever sourness is required in a dish, it is usual to add tomatoes. This may seem strange to us in the Western world where tomatoes are usually sweet, but the variety that is grown in India has a very sour taste. Unfortunately this type of tomato is not usually available in the West and so it is necessary to use vinegar to obtain the sharp flavour, whilst using the tomatoes to retain the consistency.

Note When selecting a cabbage for this dish choose one of the firm, tightly closed varieties.

IMPERIAL/METRIC	AMERICAN
4 oz./100 g. carrots	$\frac{1}{4}$ lb. carrots
8 oz./225 g. firm tomatoes	$\frac{1}{2}$ lb. firm tomatoes
6 oz./175 g. ghee	$\frac{3}{4}$ cup ghee
1$\frac{1}{2}$ tablespoons vinegar	2 tablespoons vinegar
2 oz./50 g. sugar	$\frac{1}{4}$ cup sugar
1$\frac{1}{2}$ teaspoons salt	1$\frac{1}{2}$ teaspoons salt
1$\frac{1}{2}$ teaspoons cornflour	1$\frac{1}{2}$ teaspoons cornstarch
12 oz./350 g. cabbage	$\frac{3}{4}$ lb. cabbage

1 Grate the carrots and slice the tomatoes. Fry in approximately half the ghee until tender. This should take about 5 minutes.

2 Now rub through a sieve into a large saucepan and add the vinegar, sugar, and salt.

3 Make the cornflour into a paste with a little water and add to the pan. Bring to the boil, stirring constantly. You have now made the sweet and sour sauce.

4 Wash the cabbage well and separate the leaves, cutting into 1-inch strips. Melt the rest of the ghee on a hot flame and fry the strips of cabbage for 5 minutes until tender. Use a large frying pan for this.

5 Now pour the sauce over the cabbage and boil for a further 2 minutes and serve.

Murgh palak (page 66), and baigan boortha (page 55)

I always feel that this dish is best taken on a cold winter's night as it really does warm the 'cockles of your heart'.

IMPERIAL/METRIC	AMERICAN
1 oz./25 g. tamarind	1 oz. tamarind
¼ pint/1½ dl. water	⅔ cup water
1 teaspoon chilli powder	1 teaspoon chili powder
1½ teaspoons coriander powder	1½ teaspoons coriander powder
1 cauliflower	1 cauliflower
2 oz./50 g. desiccated coconut	⅔ cup shredded coconut
¼ pint/1½ dl. milk	⅔ cup milk
½ teaspoon salt	½ teaspoon salt

1 Soak the tamarind for approximately 4 hours in the water.

2 When this has been done, squeeze out the husk and retain only the water.

3 Now place this water in a heavy saucepan and mix in the chilli powder and coriander powder.

4 Wash the cauliflower well and remove all bruises and blemishes and divide into small sprigs. Add to the pot and begin to cook on a low heat.

5 Now take the desiccated coconut and add to the milk, mixing well and pour the mixture into the saucepan.

6 Add the salt, cover and simmer gently for 20 minutes. It is important to ensure that the mixture does not dry up during cooking. Add a little water if necessary. Occasionally turn the cauliflower to ensure that the spices permeate well.

CACHUMBER

Cachumber is basically an Indian way of dressing up a salad. It makes use of ginger and raw onion to provide a piquant flavour. It is customary to have cachumber with the main course in any meal, just as in the West people take a side salad. To those unused to eating Indian food it provides a cool refreshment to a hot curry. There are no rules for making cachumber – the following recipe may be added to or subtracted from depending on the vegetables available.

IMPERIAL/METRIC	AMERICAN
2 oz./50 g. fresh ginger or 1 oz./25 g. ground ginger	3 tablespoons chopped fresh ginger or ¼ cup ground ginger
1 small onion	1 small onion
juice 2 lemons	juice 2 lemons
1½ teaspoons salt	1½ teaspoons salt
8 oz./225 g. tomatoes	½ lb. tomatoes
2 tablespoons olive oil	3 tablespoons olive oil
1 tablespoon vinegar	1½ tablespoons vinegar

1 Scrape the ginger and slice it finely, add to the onion with the lemon juice and salt. Mix well.

2 Chop the tomatoes coarsely and add to the onion, turn well and gradually pour in the oil and vinegar.

3 Leave refrigerated in an airtight container until needed for use. Cachumber is always best when chilled and straight from the fridge.

Illustrated on page 52.

HYDERABAD CHICKEN CURRY

This chicken curry differs from the conventional one in as much as it makes use of sliced coconut to give it a flavour and texture peculiar to the Deccan area of India. The Deccan is situated to the south of the western region and many famous dishes have originated around this area. This chicken curry is somewhat sweeter than usual due to the addition of the tomato purée. As with the chicken curry given in the north India section the most important part of cooking this dish is to ensure that when the chicken is finally added, it is cooked gently until tender. If in doubt about the tenderness remember it is always better to let this type of curry cook for longer and thereby ensure a tender, well-cooked dish.

IMPERIAL/METRIC	AMERICAN
1 large onion	1 large onion
2 oz./50 g. ghee	$\frac{1}{4}$ cup ghee
2 cloves garlic	2 cloves garlic
2 cardamoms	2 cardamoms
2 cloves	2 cloves
2-inch/5-cm. stick cinnamon	2-inch stick cinnamon
2 teaspoons garam masala	2 teaspoons garam masala
1 teaspoon chilli powder	1 teaspoon chili powder
1 3-lb./1$\frac{1}{3}$-kg. oven-ready chicken	1 3-lb. oven-ready chicken
4 oz./100 g. tomato purée	$\frac{2}{3}$ cup tomato paste
$\frac{1}{2}$ pint/3 dl. water	1$\frac{1}{4}$ cups water
$\frac{1}{2}$ coconut	$\frac{1}{2}$ coconut
For garnish	
1 lemon	1 lemon

1 Slice the onion and fry for 2 or 3 minutes in the ghee, together with the sliced garlic, the cardamoms, cloves, cinnamon, garam masala and chilli powder. Stir well for 5 minutes. Leave to simmer for 5 to 10 minutes on a low heat.

2 Meanwhile, skin and joint the chicken. Add together with the tomato purée. Increase the heat and turn the chicken well.

3 Turn the heat down and add the hot water.

4 Scrape out the meat of the coconut in as large chunks as possible and slice thinly. Add to the pot and cover closely; simmer for an hour until the chicken is tender.

5 Just before serving sprinkle shredded whole lemon over the top.

MURGH PALAK

This dish is really a Punjabi method of cooking although this *palak* style is found all over the west of India. Palak means anything cooked with spinach.

IMPERIAL/METRIC	AMERICAN
1 3-lb./1$\frac{1}{3}$-kg. oven-ready chicken	1 3-lb. oven-ready chicken
2 large onions	2 large onions
vegetable oil	vegetable oil
1 clove garlic	1 clove garlic
1 large tomato	1 large tomato
2 cloves	2 cloves
pinch salt	pinch salt
$\frac{1}{2}$ teaspoon coriander powder	$\frac{1}{2}$ teaspoon coriander powder
3 tablespoons milk	scant $\frac{1}{4}$ cup milk
8 oz./225 g. frozen leaf spinach	1 $\frac{1}{2}$-lb. package frozen leaf spinach
For garnish	
fresh coriander	fresh coriander
lemon	lemon

1 Skin and joint the chicken.

2 Peel and chop the onions finely and fry in a little vegetable oil for 10 minutes.

3 Now crush the garlic and chop the tomato and add together with the cloves, salt and coriander to the onions for a further 5 minutes and then add the milk and spinach. It is essential to keep turning the spinach to ensure that it is all cooked.

4 Now add the chicken pieces and cover the pot with a tightly fitting lid and cook on a very low heat for approximately 1$\frac{1}{2}$ hours until the chicken is tender.

5 Garnish with coriander leaves and lemon.

Illustrated on page 64.

No recipe book would be complete without this famous Parsee Indian dish which has become well known throughout the Western world as the chicken dish with lentils, served in Indian restaurants. The word 'dhansak' means wealthy, and thus a dhansak is a very special dish. However, in the Western world it would not be considered so special as it can be made using fatty meat from the cheaper cuts, the best being the breast of lamb. To make a good dhansak is rather complicated, and I have found in my research there are numerous recipes. I have tried to select one which is clear and easy to follow.

IMPERIAL/METRIC	AMERICAN
6 oz./175 g. chenna dal	¾ cup chenna dal
6 oz./175 g. moong dal	¾ cup moong dal
1½ pints/¾ litre water	3¾ cups water
2 large onions	2 large onions
6 oz./175 g. ghee	¾ cup ghee
2 cloves	2 cloves
3 cloves garlic	3 cloves garlic
1 teaspoon ground ginger	1 teaspoon ground ginger
1 teaspoon garam masala	1 teaspoon garam masala
1½ lb./675 g. chicken joints	1½ lb. chicken joints
1 medium aubergine	1 medium eggplant
2 large tomatoes	2 large tomatoes
8 oz./225 g. frozen spinach	½-lb. package frozen spinach
2 teaspoons salt	2 teaspoons salt

1 Wash the dals well and mix together. Place both in a large saucepan and cover with the water. Boil gently for 15 minutes.

2 Meanwhile, take another heavy pot, slice the onions and fry in the ghee for 5 minutes, then add the cloves, sliced garlic, ground ginger and garam masala.

3 Now take the thawed chicken joints and sauté for a minute on a very high flame, in this ghee, remove, drain and keep on one side.

4 Now cut the aubergine and tomatoes into 1-inch pieces and add with the spinach to the ghee. Cook for 10 minutes.

5 The lentils should by now be quite well cooked; mash them with their water to form a sauce and pour in the vegetables from the other saucepan. Stir in well until you have a thick stew.

6 Now add the sauted chicken joints and salt, cover with a lid and cook on a low heat until the chicken falls off the bone easily.

MEEN MOLI

This is a Goanese dish, which may be used for either chicken or duck. If you are using duck be sure to reduce the amount of cooking oil used, as, coupled with the natural greasiness of the duck, the dish could become unbearably oily.

IMPERIAL/METRIC	AMERICAN
1 3-lb./1⅓-kg. oven-ready chicken or duck	1 3-lb. oven-ready chicken or duck
vegetable oil	vegetable oil
2 large onions	2 large onions
3 green chillis	3 green chilis
3 cloves garlic	3 cloves garlic
4 tablespoons garam masala	⅓ cup garam masala
½ pint/3 dl. vinegar	1¼ cups vinegar
For garnish	
tomato	tomato
lemon	lemon

1 Skin and joint the bird and fry the pieces in a little oil until golden brown. Put to one side.

2 Slice the onions and chillis and fry with the garlic for 5 minutes.

3 Add the garam masala to the vinegar to form a paste and pour into the pan. Fry for a further 8 minutes.

4 Now add the meat and turn well, cover and cook on a low heat until tender.

5 Serve garnished with tomato and lemon.

Saag prawn epitomises the way the Indians have mastered the cooking of different flavours. On one hand you have one of the best seafoods and on the other a leafy vegetable, both with their own particular delicate taste. The Indian chefs have managed to produce dishes such as saag prawn which enhance both flavours with a delicate and not over heavy spicing. I am sure you will find when you have tried this dish that you will agree with me that you can taste both spinach and prawns.

IMPERIAL/METRIC	AMERICAN
1 lb./450 g. frozen leaf spinach	1 1-lb. package frozen leaf spinach
1 large onion	1 large onion
2 cloves garlic	2 cloves garlic
2 large tomatoes	2 large tomatoes
2 oz./50 g. ghee	$\frac{1}{4}$ cup ghee
$\frac{1}{2}$ teaspoon turmeric	$\frac{1}{2}$ teaspoon turmeric
$\frac{1}{2}$ teaspoon garam masala	$\frac{1}{2}$ teaspoon garam masala
$\frac{1}{2}$ teaspoon coriander powder	$\frac{1}{2}$ teaspoon coriander powder
1 teaspoon chilli powder	1 teaspoon chili powder
$\frac{1}{2}$ teaspoon ground ginger	$\frac{1}{2}$ teaspoon ground ginger
2 teaspoons sugar	2 teaspoons sugar
1-inch/2·5-cm. stick cinnamon	1-inch stick cinnamon
$\frac{1}{2}$ teaspoon salt	$\frac{1}{2}$ teaspoon salt
1 lb./450 g. prawns (shelled weight)	2 cups peeled shrimp

For garnish

lemon	lemon

1 Take the spinach and chop coarsely.

2 Now slice the onion finely with the garlic and tomatoes. Melt the ghee in a frying pan and fry the onion for 5 minutes with the garlic, then add the spinach and fry for 10 minutes, turning constantly to ensure that none of it sticks to the pan.

3 Add the tomatoes, turmeric, garam masala, coriander and chilli powder, ginger, sugar, cinnamon and salt. Simmer with a tightly-fitting lid for 15 minutes.

4 Now add the prawns and cook for 10 minutes or longer if fresh.

5 Serve garnished with lemon.

BOMBAY EEL CURRY

If you happen to live in an area where eels abound this is the Indian dish for you! I have always thought there was not much you could do with eels apart from jelly them but having tasted this particular dish I find, as with other seemingly unappetising items that the Indian treatment certainly can do a lot for even the most lowly dish. I am told that the best eels to use are the freshwater variety that do not exceed $\frac{3}{4}$ inch in diameter so do not try to use conger eel for your curry!

IMPERIAL/METRIC	AMERICAN
1 small onion	1 small onion
1 clove garlic	1 clove garlic
2 oz./50 g. ghee	$\frac{1}{4}$ cup ghee
1 teaspoon coriander powder	1 teaspoon coriander powder
1 teaspoon ground ginger	1 teaspoon ground ginger
1 teaspoon garam masala	1 teaspoon garam masala
1 teaspoon chilli powder	1 teaspoon chili powder
1$\frac{1}{2}$ lb./675 g. fresh eel	1$\frac{1}{2}$ lb. fresh eel
2 oz./50 g. tomato purée	scant $\frac{1}{4}$ cup tomato paste
1 teaspoon salt	1 teaspoon salt
lemon juice (optional)	lemon juice (optional)

1 Slice the onion and garlic and fry for 2 minutes, then add the coriander powder, ground ginger, garam masala and chilli powder. Cook for a further 5 minutes.

2 Meanwhile, wash the eels and cut into 2-inch lengths. Be sure to remove all the slime and discard the head section.

3 Now return to the pot and gradually add the tomato purée to the frying onions and garlic. Add a little water to form a thick gravy and the salt. At this stage you can if you like add some lemon juice.

4 Finally add the chopped eels. Do not cover the pan; simmer gently for 30 minutes until the fish is cooked right through, shaking the pan occasionally. Do not stir as the skins may break and the fish become mushy.

GOL GUPPAS

Another favourite western India teatime snack is a gol guppa. It is very difficult to describe it to someone who has never had a gol guppa. There is no counterpart in any other cuisine. Traditionally gol guppas have always been sold on the sea-shore on the beach at Bombay, usually with zeera pani, tamarind water. The gol guppa is roughly one inch in diameter and wafer thin. In India people eat them as one eats chips or crisps in the West. Gol guppas are easily made but must be eaten freshly cooked. They are also easily made in quantity and are therefore ideal for a party.

IMPERIAL/METRIC	AMERICAN
4 oz./100 g. plain flour	1 cup all-purpose flour
4 oz./100 g. semolina	$\frac{2}{3}$ cup semolina
4 oz./100 g. urhard dal	$\frac{1}{2}$ cup urhard dal
$\frac{1}{4}$ pint/1$\frac{1}{2}$ dl. water	$\frac{2}{3}$ cup water
ghee for frying	ghee for frying

1 Sieve the flour and semolina into a bowl. Reduce the urhad dal to a powder in a coffee grinder and add to the bowl.

2 Form into a hard dough, using the water. Knead for 15 minutes; set aside in a wet cloth for 20 minutes.

3 Divide the dough into small pieces about the size of a gooseberry, roll into small balls, using the hands, and then roll out flat as thinly as possible, dusting whenever necessary with a little flour.

4 Heat the ghee and deep-fry the gol guppas for about 2 minutes until they puff up.

5 Remove and place on kitchen tissue.

6 Serve cold with zeera pani which is made in the following way.

ZEERA PANI

IMPERIAL/METRIC	AMERICAN
4 oz./100 g. tamarind	4 oz. tamarind
1 pint/6 dl. water	2$\frac{1}{2}$ cups water
2 teaspoons cummin seed	2 teaspoons cummin seed
1 teaspoon paprika	1 teaspoon paprika pepper
4 teaspoons salt	4 teaspoons salt
2 teaspoons sugar	2 teaspoons sugar
2 pints/generous litre water	2$\frac{1}{2}$ pints water
$\frac{1}{2}$ lemon	$\frac{1}{2}$ lemon

1 Soak the tamarind overnight in the water.

2 Strain and add the remaining ingredients and the juice of the half lemon.

3 Mix well and leave for 2 hours in the fridge.

4 To fill gol guppas make a small hole in the top of each one with a finger and arrange on a dish. Pour the zeera pani into each one of them and serve.

This is another Goanese dish, basically a pancake filled with a spiced coconut mixture. It is a very good dish to serve as a teatime snack.

IMPERIAL/METRIC	AMERICAN
6 oz./175 g. plain flour	1½ cups all-purpose flour
½ teaspoon salt	½ teaspoon salt
2 eggs	2 eggs
1 pint/6 dl. milk	2½ cups milk
For filling	
2 oz./50 g. sugar	4 tablespoons sugar
2 teaspoons treacle	2 teaspoons molasses
6 oz./175 g. desiccated coconut	2 cups shredded coconut
2 teaspoons ground ginger	2 teaspoons ground ginger
2 drops aniseed essence	2 drops aniseed extract
For garnish	
icing sugar	confectioners' sugar
wedges of lemon	wedges of lemon

1 Sieve the flour into a large bowl, together with the salt, and beat in the eggs and milk until well blended. Allow this batter to stand for 30 minutes.

2 Meanwhile, prepare the stuffing by mixing the sugar and molasses in a bowl and adding the coconut, ground ginger and aniseed essence and mixing well. Leave this on one side.

3 Now take a heavy omelette pan and melt just enough ghee to cover the bottom of the frying pan. Pour in 2 tablespoons of the batter with a small ladle, tip the pan to spread the batter evenly over the surface and cook for approximately a minute on a moderate heat until the pancake begins to brown, turn the pancake over and cook the other side for a minute. Remove from the heat and keep on a warm plate and cook the rest of the pancakes using a little bit of the ghee each time.

4 Put approximately a tablespoon of the mixture in the centre of the pancake and roll up.

5 Arrange each of the alebele on the plate. Dust with icing sugar and serve cold, garnished with wedges of lemon.

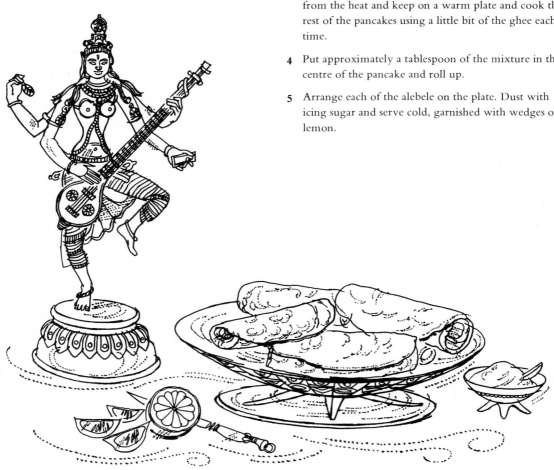

Jallebi are those crisp, round whirls that one sees on sale in Indian grocers. They are far too sticky for my liking but I know that a great many people like this sweet. Actually, I must confess that I like jallebis so long as they are freshly made but usually those on sale have been lying around longer than the couple of hours necessary to ensure freshness. However, it is very easy to make them at home as no special ingredients are necessary at all.

IMPERIAL/METRIC	AMERICAN
12 oz./350 g. plain flour	3 cups all-purpose flour
cold water to mix	cold water to mix
$\frac{1}{4}$ pint/1$\frac{1}{2}$ dl. yogurt	$\frac{2}{3}$ cup yogurt
1 oz./25 g. dried yeast	2 cakes compressed yeast
1 lb./450 g. sugar	2 cups sugar
1 pint/6 dl. water	2$\frac{1}{2}$ cups water
pinch saffron	pinch saffron
6 cardamoms	6 cardamoms
6 cloves	6 cloves
vegetable oil	vegetable oil
	For garnish
icing sugar	confectioners' sugar

1 Sieve the flour into a bowl and add sufficient cold water along with the yogurt and yeast to form a batter the consistency of double cream. Cover and stand in a warm place for about 4 hours to ferment.

2 Meanwhile prepare the syrup by dissolving the sugar in the pint of water in a saucepan, together with the saffron, cardamoms and cloves. Bring to the boil and evaporate until a heavy syrup is obtained.

3 Now take a medium deep frying pan and fill with oil; heat to nearly boiling. Take the batter and using either an icing bag or a narrow funnel, allow the batter to run into the hot oil to form the traditional figure eights or double circle whirls. Cook for about a minute, turning constantly, until the jallebi is a light brown colour.

4 Remove, drain and immerse in the syrup for approximately 5 minutes, so that the syrup runs through the pipes of the jallebi without making the crisp outside become soggy.

5 Remove from the syrup, drain and dust with icing sugar. There is no doubt that you will be the envy of all your friends when you produce home-made jallebis at teatime.

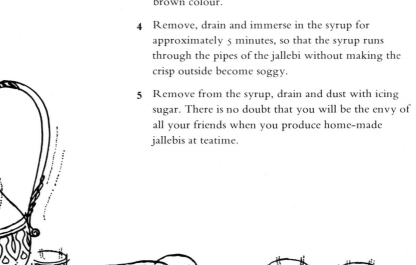

Chaat is the name given to any fresh fruit salad spiced with chillis, salt, lemon juice and red peppers. It is very popular in the afternoons when tea is taken, as although it seems strange, the hot spices coupled with the fresh fruit allay the effects of the afternoon heat. Even in the West there is nothing quite so refreshing as a bowl of refrigerated chaat. The following recipe is for a basic chaat using readily available fruits. However, you can use whatever fruit you can lay your hands on, but if they are too juicy or ripe the effect of the chaat will be spoilt. In fact, in India it is quite a common practice to use unripe fruit when making chaat.

IMPERIAL/METRIC	AMERICAN
8 oz./225 g. mandarin oranges	½ lb. mandarin oranges
8 oz./225 g. apples	½ lb. apples
8 oz./225 g. bananas	½ lb. bananas
8 oz./225 g. guavas	½ lb. guavas
8 oz./225 g. pears	½ lb. pears
4 oz./100 g. stoned cherries	¼ lb. pitted cherries
2 tablespoons lemon juice	3 tablespoons lemon juice
2 teaspoons sugar	2 teaspoons sugar
1 teaspoon chilli powder	1 teaspoon chili powder
1 teaspoon paprika	1 teaspoon paprika pepper
1 teaspoon salt	1 teaspoon salt
1½ teaspoons ground ginger	1½ teaspoons ground ginger
1 teaspoon garam masala	1 teaspoon garam masala

1 Peel the oranges, apples and bananas, and chop coarsely with the guavas, pears and cherries, taking care to remove the stones and pips.

2 Put the pieces of fruit in a bowl and sprinkle the lemon juice over them, mixing well.

3 Now take the sugar and spices and mix together in a dry bowl. Sprinkle these over the fruit pieces, ensuring that it is all well covered.

4 Refrigerate for approximately an hour before serving.

Illustrated on page 28.

PISTA KULFI
Pistachio ice cream

This is probably the best ice cream I have ever tasted and I know that anything that contains pistachios is bound to delight the palate.

IMPERIAL/METRIC	AMERICAN
12-oz./350-g. can condensed milk	¾ pint condensed milk
½ pint/3 dl. double cream	1¼ cups heavy cream
4 oz./100 g. castor sugar	½ cup sugar
2 eggs	2 eggs
2 drops almond essence	2 drops almond extract
2 drops green food colouring	2 drops green food coloring
4 oz./100 g. pistachios	scant cup pistachios

1 Heat the condensed milk in a saucepan and add the double cream with the sugar.

2 Separate the egg whites and beat until they form peaks.

3 Beat the yolks into the milk together with the almond essence and the green colouring. Allow this mixture to simmer gently.

4 Meanwhile, soak the shelled pistachios to make it easy to remove the skins. Chop finely and add to the saucepan, beating in well. Bring to the boil and then refrigerate until the mixture is nearly set.

5 Remove and fold in the beaten egg whites. Beat well and freeze until firm.

Note To make the dish authentic the ice cream should be frozen in the traditional aluminium cone shapes used by the kulfi wallahs.

Illustrated on page 61.

BOMBAY HALWA

Over the ages different styles of cuisine grow up around different cities and it is usual that each city has dishes named after it. One of the specific groups of dishes is the 'halwa' dishes and we find many varying types of halwa, each purporting to come from a different city. Thus we have Karachi halwa, Dacca halwa and probably the most famous, Bombay halwa. Halwas differ from the standard style of Indian sweet in as much as they are not based entirely on milk. Bombay halwas contain no milk whatsoever. It is, however, reasonably easy to prepare, but do not expect to emulate exactly the 'halwai's' art as I am positive that this is one dish you have to be born into!

IMPERIAL/METRIC	AMERICAN
12 oz./350 g. sugar	1½ cups sugar
½ pint/3 dl. water	1¼ cups water
2 oz./50 g. cornflour	½ cup cornstarch
juice 1 lemon	juice 1 lemon
4 oz./100 g. unsalted butter	½ cup sweet butter
2 oz./50 g. cashew nuts	½ cup cashew nuts
2 oz./50 g. almonds	½ cup almonds
2 oz./50 g. pistachios	½ cup pistachios
2 cardamoms	2 cardamoms

1 Dissolve the sugar in a saucepan with the water over a low heat. Bring to the boil and boil for approximately 10 minutes.

2 Meanwhile, remove some of the sugar solution and mix with the cornflour to form a paste; add to the rest of the solution, stirring continuously.

3 Now add the lemon juice and a little of the butter. Continue to cook on a medium heat until the mixture separates.

4 Meanwhile, chop the nuts and crush the cardamoms and add. Pour into a fudge tray and allow to cool.

5 When cold, cut into the traditional diamond shapes. Halwa will keep indefinitely in an airtight tin. It makes very suitable presents for your friends.

PODINA KA SHARBAT

In India mint forms the basis of a very tasty, cooling beverage. It is essential to use fresh mint when making podina ka sharbat as dried mint does not have the same intensity of flavour.

IMPERIAL/METRIC	AMERICAN
4 oz./100 g. fresh mint	3 cups chopped fresh mint
½ teaspoon ground ginger	½ teaspoon ground ginger
6 oz./175 g. sugar	¾ cup sugar
1 tablespoon lemon juice	1½ tablespoons lemon juice
1½ pints/¾ litre water	3¾ cups water
For garnish	
fresh mint	fresh mint

1 Crush the mint leaves, preferably with a mortar and pestle, but failing that with a liquidiser or coffee grinder, add the ground ginger, sugar and lemon juice along with the water.

2 Then transfer to a liquidiser and liquidise for 5 minutes.

3 Strain through a fine cloth, repeating if necessary to obtain a clear green liquid. Podina ka sharbat is best served as a frappé over crushed ice.

4 Garnish with a few sprigs of fresh mint.

CONCLUSION ON WESTERN INDIA

The west Indians eat plenty of cachumber (chopped salad) with all their food. A lot of the dishes like saag prawn and murgh palak do not need extra vegetables but when entertaining the secret lies in preparing small amounts of different dishes so that your guests can have as much variety as possible. It will be worth trying the Bombay eel curry although it may sound a little off-putting at first. For a cocktail party pre-prepared chaat served in little bowls from the fridge is very good in the height of summer as a sweet dish.

CENTRAL INDIA

The preceding chapters have covered the extremities of India; there remains one chapter to cover what I will call central India, which centres around Delhi. Whilst there is a definite 'Delhi' style of cooking, the cuisine of central India tends to be very cosmopolitan, taking dishes from all parts of India and indeed, from other countries. Included in this chapter are those recipes which I consider to be universal throughout India and which have had their regional origins obscured by the passage of time. The region of central India includes such famous names as Fatehpur-Sikri, Jaipur, Agra and Lucknow, all names of beautiful Indian cities which have existed for centuries, all producing dishes to delight the palate.

DUM ARVI

This recipe makes use of yams, a vegetable very common throughout India and the West Indies. For general use, yams are prepared in a similar way to potatoes, but as they tend to be a little more glutinous and starchy it is necessary, after having peeled the yams, to soak them for about an hour in salted water to remove the excess starch. In central India where yams grow quite abundantly the yam will often take the place of rice in a meal. It is only fair to warn you that when selecting yams in a European grocer's it is essential to make sure that the yams are not bruised or damaged; choose only the firm ones.

IMPERIAL/METRIC	AMERICAN
1 lb/450 g. yams	1 lb. yams
4 oz./100 g. ghee	$\frac{1}{2}$ cup ghee
1 small onion	1 small onion
$\frac{1}{2}$ teaspoon ground ginger	$\frac{1}{2}$ teaspoon ground ginger
1 teaspoon coriander powder	1 teaspoon coriander powder
$\frac{1}{2}$ teaspoon garam masala	$\frac{1}{2}$ teaspoon garam masala
$\frac{1}{2}$ teaspoon paprika	$\frac{1}{2}$ teaspoon paprika pepper
2 teaspoons salt	2 teaspoons salt
2 green chillis	2 green chilis
For garnish	
chopped parsley	chopped parsley
little butter	little butter

1 Wash and peel the yams and soak for an hour in salted water. Remove and wash off the jelly-like outer coating that forms and dry them off in a tea-towel. Chop roughly into 1-inch cubes.

2 Fry in the ghee. Remove and place to one side.

3 Slice the onion and fry in the remaining ghee. Then stir in the ground ginger, coriander powder, garam masala, paprika, salt and the chopped green chillis.

4 Cover with a loose-fitting lid and place in a medium oven (375°F., Gas Mark 4–5) for 1 hour. After this the yams should be almost dry and beautifully tender.

5 Serve garnished with chopped parsley and a little butter.

BAIGAN BHUGIA

A bhugia is the name given to any vegetable dish cooked without any water. This means the dish calls for some care in preparation and that the final result is very dry. Any number of different types of vegetable can be used in a bhugia and the following recipe makes use of two vegetables, the green pepper or pimento and aubergines. Because of the dryness of the vegetable it tends to be rather hot but of course you can control this by altering the amount of paprika or chillis you include.

IMPERIAL/METRIC	AMERICAN
2 oz./50 g. ghee	¼ cup ghee
1 large onion	1 large onion
8 oz./225 g. aubergines	½ lb. eggplants
8 oz./225 g. green peppers	½ lb. green sweet peppers
1½ teaspoons salt	1½ teaspoons salt
1 teaspoon paprika	1 teaspoon paprika pepper
2 small green chillis	2 small green chilis
2 oz./50 g. tomato purée	scant ¼ cup tomato paste
1 teaspoon garam masala	1 teaspoon garam masala

1 Heat the ghee in a heavy saucepan and add the coarsely chopped onion.

2 Take the aubergines (they should be of the long variety) and remove the leafy stem and cut into ½-inch cubes.

3 Cut the green peppers in half and remove the seeds and chop coarsely. Add, with the aubergine, to the onion and cook for 5 minutes, stirring constantly.

4 Now add the salt, paprika and chillis. Cover and simmer for a further 10 minutes.

5 Stir in the tomato purée and the garam masala and simmer for another 5 minutes.

RAETA

Whenever I am asked to recommend a suitable antidote to a hot curry I always come up with raeta. Raeta is the general name for any yogurt-based cooked vegetable or fruit dish which is served to accompany a meal, preferably chilled. There is no limit to the many different varieties that can be made. The most popular recipes make use of bananas, potatoes, raw aubergines and mint, to name but a few. But the one form of raeta that has become most famous through its ubiquitous presence on the menus of all Indian restaurants in the West is cucumber raeta. It is difficult to give a recipe for this as the proportions of cucumber to yogurt vary with the individual taste, but the following recipe is the way that I prefer it.

IMPERIAL/METRIC	AMERICAN
1-inch/2·5-cm length cucumber	1-inch length cucumber
½ pint/3 dl. yogurt	1¼ cups yogurt
½ teaspoon salt	½ teaspoon salt
For garnish	
½ teaspoon paprika	½ teaspoon paprika pepper
1 teaspoon dried mint	1 teaspoon dried mint

1 Slice the cucumber in the normal way and cut each slice into narrow strips or dice.

2 Mix these strips into the yogurt with the salt.

3 Finally sprinkle with the mint and paprika.

4 Serve chilled in large quantities.

Illustrated on page 17.

A foogath is the name given to a dish which utilises pre-cooked vegetables. It is therefore a very good way of using up the greens from a Sunday roast, and it is one of the quickest methods of 'currying-up' a vegetable.

IMPERIAL/METRIC	AMERICAN
1 large onion	1 large onion
2 cloves garlic	2 cloves garlic
2 green chillis	2 green chilis
4 oz./100 g. ghee	½ cup ghee
1 lb./450 g. cooked cabbage	1 lb. cooked cabbage
1 teaspoon garam masala	1 teaspoon garam masala
1 teaspoon salt	1 teaspoon salt
For garnish	
desiccated coconut	shredded coconut

1 Slice the onion and fry together with the sliced garlic and green chillis in the ghee until the onions are golden brown.

2 Now add the cabbage with the garam masala, ground ginger and salt and stir on a medium heat until the cabbage is heated right through and becomes very dry.

3 Serve garnished with desiccated coconut.

MUTTON DOPIAZAH

A dopiazah is any dish which contains a large proportion of onions. There are many schools of thought as to how much onion there should actually be; some say it should be equal in weight to the meat or main constituent or double the amount of meat, or any fraction between the two. This is entirely up to the individual cook. The essential requirement is that some of the onion should be fried at the beginning and some added raw when the mutton has been half cooked. This recipe is for mutton dopiazah, by adaptation one can use the same recipe for beef or chicken.

IMPERIAL/METRIC	AMERICAN
1 lb./450 g. onions	1 lb. onions
6 oz./175 g. ghee	¾ cup ghee
1 lb./450 g. mutton	1 lb. mutton
1 teaspoon chilli powder	1 teaspoon chili powder
½ pint/3 dl. yogurt	1¼ cups yogurt
½ teaspoon ground ginger	½ teaspoon ground ginger
1 teaspoon salt	1 teaspoon salt
2 cloves garlic	2 cloves garlic
4 cardamoms	4 cardamoms
1 teaspoon garam masala	1 teaspoon garam masala
½ teaspoon cummin seed	½ teaspoon cummin seed

1 Slice the onions thinly and fry half of them in the ghee until golden brown. Remove from the ghee and set to one side.

2 Now take the mutton cut into 1-inch cubes (shoulder is probably best) and sauté in the ghee until sealed on both sides. Remove the meat and set aside.

3 Now add the chilli powder and remaining onions along with the yogurt, ginger and salt. Cook for 2 minutes and add the meat. Cover and simmer for 10 minutes.

4 Crush the garlic and add this to the saucepan (it may be necessary to add some water to prevent the mixture from becoming too dry), then add the browned onions, cardamoms, garam masala and cummin seed. Cover and simmer for 30 minutes.

Note Dopiazah has an interesting sweet, hot taste which varies according to the amount of onions used.

KEEMA KARELA

Karela is the name given to a particular relative of the cucumber and courgette family which is known as bitter gourd. To prepare a dish from such an unlikely vegetable may sound a little strange at first, and I must confess that to the unschooled palate the taste of keema karela does not always evoke cries of ecstacy. Once the taste has been acquired, however, there is no doubt that most people become hooked on this dish. As with dum arvi, it provides a good opportunity to use an unusual and exotic vegetable. Karela can usually be found in cans at most Indian and Continental grocers. Since fresh karela is difficult to come by this recipe makes use of the canned vegetable.

IMPERIAL/METRIC	AMERICAN
6 oz./175 g. ghee	¾ cup ghee
1 8-oz./225-g. can karela	1 8-oz. can karela
2 large onions	2 large onions
1½ teaspoons salt	1½ teaspoons salt
1 teaspoon ground black pepper	1 teaspoon ground black pepper
½ teaspoon cummin seed powder	½ teaspoon cummin seed powder
1 teaspoon garam masala	1 teaspoon garam masala
1-inch/2·5-cm. stick cinnamon	1-inch stick cinnamon
2 lb./900 g. raw minced meat	2 lb. raw ground meat
For garnish	
tomato	tomato
wedges of lemon	wedges of lemon

1 Canned karelas are usually immersed in brine so you will have to drain off the brine before cooking. You will notice that there are a lot of fawn-coloured seeds. These must not be discarded on any account. Cut the karelas into strips.

2 Heat the ghee in a heavy pan until it is smoking. Reduce heat and fry the strips of karela for about 2 minutes. Drain and remove the karelas to a warm dish.

3 Now slice the onions and fry until golden brown. Add the salt, black pepper, cummin seed powder, garam masala and the stick of cinnamon and simmer for 5 minutes on a gentle heat.

4 As with keema pimento in Chapter 1, the most important part of making this dish is the cooking of the minced meat. If the minced meat has been standing and is moist, drain off any excess blood and put the minced meat into the saucepan. Maintain a low heat and stir constantly until it is cooked. Make sure none sticks to the bottom of the pan. Lastly add the karela.

5 Serve garnished with tomato and wedges of lemon.

PHIRNI

Phirni is a very popular sweet and can best be described as a blancmange. It makes use of almonds and pistachios and kewra essence. These give a distinctive Indian flavour. The only difficult ingredient here is rice flour which can be bought from most Indian delicatessens. However, it would probably be better to use whole rice and grind it yourself as you are sure of the quality of the rice that you are using when you do this.

IMPERIAL/METRIC	AMERICAN
1 oz./25 g. rice	2 tablespoons rice
¼ pint/1½ dl. water	⅔ cup water
1 pint/6 dl. milk	2½ cups milk
4 oz./100 g. sugar	½ cup sugar
5 drops kewra essence	5 drops kewra extract
1 oz./25 g. mixed pistachios and almonds	scant ¼ cup pistachios and almonds
For garnish	
almonds	almonds
pistachios	pistachios

1 Soak the rice for 1½ hours then drain and grind into a paste with the water.

2 Heat the milk slowly in a saucepan and stir in the rice paste. Stir until the mixture begins to thicken. Remove from the heat and add the sugar.

3 When the sugar is fully dissolved, bring to the boil and simmer for 2 minutes. Now allow to cool and add the kewra essence and the chopped almonds and pistachios.

4 Serve chilled either in individual dishes or in a central dish garnished with split almonds and pistachios.

ALOO KA MITTHAI

Unlike most of the preceding recipes for Indian sweets this one utilises dried instead of fresh milk. It must be stressed however, that the milk must be of the best full cream variety and is best bought in the form packed as baby food. You will also see that this dish utilises potatoes which must be the newest available. Although obviously very high in calories I am sure you will find this sweet dish quite pleasant.

IMPERIAL/METRIC	AMERICAN
2½ lb./1¼ kg. potatoes (preferably new)	2½ lb. potatoes (preferably new)
1 lb./450 g. full cream dried milk	1 lb. full cream dried milk
1 lb./450 g. sugar	2 cups sugar
8 oz./225 g. ghee	2 cups ghee
some icing sugar	some confectioners' sugar

1 Wash the potatoes and steam them for 15 minutes, remove the skins and mash.

2 Now add the dried milk and sugar and mix well. Cook gently on a very low heat, gradually adding the ghee. Keep stirring and when the ghee is all separated out, transfer to a baking tin. Allow to cool and sprinkle well with icing sugar.

3 Cut into the traditional diamond shapes and serve. This dish will keep indefinitely in an airtight container.

LUSSI

I have said before that the most popular drink that people of the Indian sub-continent usually take with their food is water, but the next most popular is a drink known as lussi. You will see this offered in the better Indian restaurants sometimes spelt on the menu as lassi, however the spelling I have given is nearest to the correct pronunciation. I must admit that this is one of these specialities for which one needs to acquire a taste and I always think it is most enjoyable taken on a very hot day. Lussi can be drunk in two ways, either sweet (meeta) or salted (numkeen). I suggest the sweet one is tried first as the salted drink is really designed for hot climates.

Note Home-made yogurt is of course the best for this but if you use shop yogurt add a little more milk.

IMPERIAL/METRIC	AMERICAN
½ pint/3 dl. yogurt	1¼ cups yogurt
½ pint/3 dl. milk	1¼ cups milk
juice 1 lemon	juice 1 lemon
½ teaspoon kewra essence	½ teaspoon kewra extract
sugar or salt to taste	sugar or salt to taste
ice cubes	ice cubes

1 Put the yogurt, milk, lemon juice and kewra essence into a liquidiser. Rose water can be used if you cannot obtain kewra essence.

2 Add some ice cubes and liquidise until the ice cubes have almost disappeared.

3 Pour into tall glasses and add the sugar or salt to taste.

4 Serve with a slice of lemon and a drinking straw.

CONCLUSION ON CENTRAL INDIA

The most famous dish from central India is the dopiazah and in my opinion if you are entertaining and trying to use authentic central Indian cuisine it should form the main dish – any of the varieties, also dum arvi. Baigan bhugia is also a good accompaniment to the dopiazah.

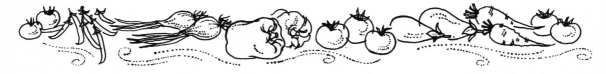

INDEX